The Secrets of
THE LENORMAND ORACLE

SYLVIE STEINBACH

ISBN: 1-4196-7030-1
ISBN-13: 978-1419670305
Library of Congress Control Number: 2007905691

Visit www.createspace.com/3330286 to order additional copies.

DEDICATION

I dedicate this Lenormand book to my aunt, a Lenormand expert and talented psychic who spent her life helping others, kindly guiding people with heart and wisdom until her last days.

Madame Paulette Steinbach Cunego

I am grateful to have found support and friendships on my path and I would like to thank:

Jean Marie Sibourg
Paul Riviere
Carol Langston
Teri Taylor
Jane Eugene Peters
Virginie Strub
Tara de Bach
And all the rest of my wonderful clients!

CONTENTS

PREFACE

Los Angeles is the capital of the NOW. Clients want to know the future in full detail all within a 15 minute session. Fast questions, fast answers! It is quite impossible to have a detailed reading in 15 minutes, and yet the reality of our fast-paced lifestyle demands precise information in a short amount of time. We live in a world of uncertainty; the demand 'to know' is a reaction to our growing insecurities, as well as to a world that seems increasingly unstable.

During the mid-1990's, the world of psychics underwent a revolution, bringing us mainstream and making us part of the services that the rich and famous utilize to navigate daily life. Psychics, like psychotherapists, massage therapists, and hypnotherapists among others, have become one more tool in the celebrity arsenal chest.

I was born in France from a lineage of Free-Masons and well-established Seers. I experienced my psychic abilities quite early. Yet, without close teachers (my parents were not tuned in), I had to initiate myself into the world of metaphysics -as most apprentices do, through books and experimentation. My psychic relatives lived far away and my visits to them were few and far between. Fortunately, during these brief encounters, I was a quick study and managed to swiftly become well-versed in manipulating pendulums and understanding tarot cards. In addition, I practiced on many other metaphysical tools used to forecast events or understand convoluted situations.

By the age of 13, I had learned the basics of the Little Lenormand deck, a divination tool well-loved on my father's side of the family. I continued to expand my metaphysical education learning spiritual astrology with the Rosicruscian organization, numerology and by studying the concepts of past life and karmic lessons to help unveil the mystical secrets of life. Well versed in esoteric knowledge I went on to host my own radio show in the South of France- *Karmic Astrology*. It was an opportunity to introduce the concepts of life purpose and past lives to an audience through the study of astrological natal charts. I mainly utilized volunteers and unveiled their life paths live on the air.

Despite the success of the show I felt that I had not achieved my full potential, so I made the biggest decision of my entire life - to venture to the United States to find my own path. I carried with me on this fortunate journey my most treasured possessions: my psychic talents and my little Lenormand cards. This leap of faith paid off a few years later as I became a successful professional psychic in Los Angeles, California. However, along the way I also encountered new challenges, many of which involved meeting the needs of an increasing demanding clientele.

The brutal reality of the psychic business in the entertainment capital was good training for me. I tackled the challenge of forecasting the future more quickly in a short session and learned to manage the pressure. In short order, I had to become as accurate as possible, as quickly as possible in order to build my reputation. Yet, if I wanted to reach new levels of accuracy, my Lenormand knowledge and understanding of it up to that point, had to be completely revamped. I knew that in order to make it as a successful Seer, to provide what my clientele was expecting, I had to deliver highly accurate readings for our modern lifestyle and I had to do this on a consistent basis - no ifs, ands or buts. I did indeed learn to be a better and faster psychic, and consequently my business flourished, and a famous and loyal clientele followed. My ability to upgrade the oracle's system to fit my clients' needs was a major factor in my professional growth.

The Little Lenormand deck - the "petit jeu" Lenormand - is one of the most popular oracles in the metaphysical world today. That being said, the Lenormand deck is quite obscure in the United

States, as its distribution is sparse. The 36 Lenormand cards created in the mid-19th Century in France by Mademoiselle Marie Anne Adelaide Lenormand appear to be at first simple and charming. Most people collect the cards for their different artworks, but often they do not know how to use their divination features, as very few Lenormand books -explaining the cards-, are available and are most likely written in French or German. No English literature has been made available and it is contributing to the scarcity of the deck in the Anglo-Saxon marketplace.

A written step-by-step guide needed to be published to help a user understand the Lenormand oracle and bring it back into the 21st Century. My updated manual with its fast-track interpretation method is the answer to this void which has plagued the Lenormand cards in the English speaking countries.

Creating this guide and sharing my extensive knowledge of the cards fell into my lap when my psychic aunt Paulette passed away and with her, 65 years of Lenormand experience. In that year I understood my responsibility to keep the legacy alive, and to pass on my expertise in an intelligible way.

The coming of age of the internet has made the Lenormand deck accessible to purchase anywhere in the world- i.e. eBay and Amazon- but to capture an international audience and prosper, the deck needs multi-lingual experts willing to teach the intricate features of the oracle to the masses. I decided to write this book to share my Lenormand secrets with anyone who is interested in understanding this amazing set of cards. I hope this educational book becomes a valuable tool for anyone searching for answers from these charming cards known as 'the Little Lenormand.'

INTRODUCTION

The Lenormand Story

The Lenormand cards were named after a famous French woman: Marie Anne Adelaide Lenormand (1772-1843), one of the most renowned psychics in history. Her life story would make an exciting period novel as she lived during some of the most tumultuous years in Europe: the French Revolution. Marie Anne Adelaide Lenormand started "reading" her peers' futures at 14 years of age, as her undeniable psychic gifts could not be repressed by her religious caretakers. At the time, the young Seer used her favorite deck of cards – an ancient tarot deck called Etteila – along with the art of palmistry. How she acquired these esoteric skills remains a mystery, as Marie Anne spent her childhood in a convent. When she reached her teens she was sent to Paris to work at the family owned shop. Her stay was a difficult period, as Marie Anne felt disenfranchised from her family heritage. However the young woman continued to hone her fortune telling craft. Unfortunately, her integration into the Parisian side of the family eventually failed so she soon departed for London, where she financially supported herself as a psychic, and pursued advanced studies in the esoteric arts.

At 25 years old, back from London, she started her "Salon" at Rue Tournon in Paris, a venue where she foretold the future to an upscale clientele. With a transfixed and cult-like following, Marie Anne reached a level of unsurpassed celebrity status. Witness to the French Revolution and aggressively involved in the political game, Mademoiselle Lenormand befriended revolutionaries and nobles both to ensure her safety as well as to move her own political agenda. A royalist believer, she was thrown in jail a number of times for practicing witchcraft and for being a traitor to the new regime. During one of her jail experiences Marie Anne made the acquaintance of Josephine de Beauharnais. The young women's friendship would become legendary; as Josephine went on to marry the unknown Napoleon Bonaparte at the beginning of his military career.

Because of this fateful connection, Bonaparte consulted the Seer several times during his ascension to power. Marie Anne's accuracy was disturbing to the future Emperor who could not believe such a woman could be so accurate. Her notoriety was such that Marie Anne soon read for Kings and Queens, and of course, her beloved friend, the Empress Josephine, who kept her very busy. Wealth, fame and favors were abundant in Lenormand's little salon. Yet, as fortune would have it, Emperor Napoleon was going mad in his quest for absolute power. He had grown to dislike the psychic talents of Marie Anne as he was coming to see them as a threat. When she foretold the desire of the monarch to divorce Josephine, Bonaparte ordered Marie Anne's arrest to ensure her silence. While she was confined, demonstrations were held to secure Marie Anne's release. After the official divorce of Napoleon and Josephine, she was set free. After this fateful turn of events, Marie Anne Adelaide Lenormand became a legend.

Lenormand's relationship with these two historical figures would continue until the demise of the Emperor and the death of Josephine, her long time friend. Marie Anne's own wealth had grown to include real estates, cash and paintings. She did some writing on her own, but without much success. There after, Marie Anne began to give exclusive teachings to selected students. As Marie Anne aged she took care of her extended family as she never married. At her death, Marie Anne was childless, and her designated heir her favorite nephew, then took over her considerable fortune. According to popular lore, during the inventory of her personal belongings, is when a little deck of 36 cards was found, named le petit Jeu.

The Little Lenormand deck called the petit Jeu was allegedly printed for the first time sometime after 1840. 36 picturesque cards in numeric order with specific symbols constitute a standard Little Lenormand. Collectors immediately started to covet the cards, even though the deck was primarily published as a divination tool. Few fortune tellers excelled at the Little Lenormand as the passing of knowledge onto the next generation was an exclusive oral rite inaugurated by Lenormand herself.

Some predictive techniques finally appeared in books written in French or Germanic languages. However, finding any understandable manuscript explaining the deck on a store shelf was like looking for a needle in a hay stack. Nevertheless, the deck's popularity flourished in Europe and today the Little Lenormand deck is a classic oracle. So how can someone find this marvelous deck?

All Little Lenormand versions published since the deck's debut are available now through the web. The internet has largely contributed to the international renaissance of the cards - new artworks, new French and German books - even though most customers still have no idea how to use them with their full features.

You will find this oracle referenced under many different names such as:
The Little Lenormand deck
Le petit Lenormand
Cartomancy deck Mlle Lenormand
Lenormand oracle

You may find out that several other Lenormand divination systems are available. The Grand Lenormand and the Lenormand Tarot are also oracles with their own interpretations. They have their own secrets that are not explained in this book dedicated only to the Little Lenormand.

I suggest you browse the different metaphysical websites, visit esoteric shops to see and feel these wonderful cards and purchase a set in order to increase your comprehension of the book. Remember that practicing with a tool accelerates the learning process. In Secret 7 of this book you will find all the information needed to find the right Little Lenormand deck for you.

SECRET 1

The Meaning of the Cards

The 36 cards represent the keyboard of a grand piano and need to be understood individually. Each symbol or picture reveals important information that one must learn in order to develop a psychic relationship with the deck. To ease your comprehension, the cards have been divided into 6 groups:

Group 1
> the horseman
> the clover
> the ship
> the house
> the tree
> the clouds

Group 2
> the snake
> the coffin
> the bouquet
> the scythe
> the whip
> the birds

Group 3
> the child
> the fox
> the bear
> the stars
> the storks
> the dog

Group 4
 the tower
 the garden
 the mountain
 the crossroad
 the mice
 the heart

Group 5
 the ring
 the book
 the letter
 the man
 the woman
 the lily

Group 6
 the sun
 the moon
 the key
 the fish
 the anchor
 the cross

In the following pages each card is explained with detailed meanings and keywords for an easier recall. Special features, footnotes and basic card associations have also been listed to facilitate spread interpretations. Your first step to study the Little Lenormand should be to practice regularly one card or two cards spreads to accelerate your memorization of the meanings. This is an excellent exercise to facilitate psychic insights.

You can "read" your own future by asking the deck simple questions such as "will I pass the final exam?" or "will I receive a raise?" but, do not overdo it, as to avoid confusing answers. Practice by focusing on the question, and then draw one or two cards and look at them quietly. Patience and internal listening are the keys to developing your skills. This exercise will not only increase your concentration, but will also make learning the cards more fun.

The first group of 6 cards:

1. The horseman: a gentleman riding a beautiful stallion across fields

2. The clover: a four leaf clover fully displayed for all to see

3. The ship: a magnificent vessel braving the vast ocean to reach land

4. The house: an elegant mansion with a rose garden in the country

5. The tree: a solid tree standing alone under the sun

6. The clouds: dark and white clouds floating in the daytime sky

1- The Horseman

Keywords/meanings:
Through the horseman new situations or people are coming toward you. It announces that news is on the way and the time reference is "soon," or "at any time." The information brings updates and feedback. The card can predict a new chapter in life. In essence, it is telling you to be prepared for a change.

Descriptions:
The symbol portrays an elegant, well-proportioned gentleman; therefore you may meet a nice looking man with possible athletic abilities who will be interesting and exciting. If the horseman relates to a woman, she will appear fit, independent and outgoing.

Astrological reference:
The ruler of the horseman is Mercury (communication).
The astrological sign is Aquarius - air element - (January 21st to February 21st).
The horseman's month is January, (1st month of the New Year).

Associated Lenormand playing card:
Nine of hearts

Special features:
The horseman indicates time frames like tomorrow, next week or next month. You should always look at the cards that follow this picture to get an idea of when the event is likely to occur. You may estimate this information by using the number on top of the card, in this case number 1. It could represent the month of January or the period falling into the Aquarius sign.

Body connection:
The horseman connects to the lower parts of the legs, specifically the feet and knees.

Card associations:
Horseman + clover (2): upcoming opportunities, second chance
Horseman + ship (3): brief visit, meeting with a foreigner, guest
Horseman + house (4): new home (rent, lease or purchase)
Horseman + tree (5): new soul mate entering your life
Horseman + clouds (6): confusing information, conflicted news
Horseman + snake (7): difficult news, challenges ahead
Horseman + coffin (8): important changes, transition period, condolences
Horseman + bouquet (9): new attractive situation, happy news, handsome man
Horseman + scythe (10): rupture, separation, news of an accident, surgeon
Horseman + whip (11): sexual encounter, lover, quarrels, fights
Horseman + birds (12): phone calls, conferences, announcements, news
Horseman + child (13): pending birth, pregnancy news, single dad, son
Horseman + fox (14): job news, new employment, new employee
Horseman + bear (15): financial information, new source of cash flow, payments
Horseman + stars (16): hope, spiritual signs, help
Horseman + storks (17): changes ahead, possible residential move
Horseman + dog (18): news from a familiar individual, visit from a friend
Horseman + tower (19): new investment property, business acquisition
Horseman + garden (20): new network of people, in-laws, guests
Horseman + mountain (21): delays ahead, slower pace, stand still
Horseman + crossroad (22): new possibilities, multiple offers, options
Horseman + mice (23): stressful times, increased pressure

Horseman + heart (24): new personal relationship, new lover, emotional intimacy

Horseman + ring (25): commitment, marriage, proposal, new contract

Horseman + book (26): new project, important information, discovery

Horseman + letter (27): mail, message, package, documents, carrier

Horseman + man (28): new gentleman coming into your life, news from a man

Horseman + woman (29): new lady entering your life, feedback from a female

Horseman + lily (30): vacation time, rest, pending retirement, peaceful period

Horseman + sun (31): success, victory, achievement, incoming fame

Horseman + moon (32): emotional happiness, new romance, new creative work

Horseman + key (33): spiritual lesson coming, turning point, significant event

Horseman + fish (34): new business endeavor, encounter with a business man

Horseman + anchor (35): stable period ahead, reassuring news

Horseman + cross (36): worries, painful news, serious concerns

Footnotes:
The horseman has a fast timetable like the moon card that translates into hours, days or weeks. New people will step into your life regardless of what you do. When this card appears, the picture announces news, a renewal of a current situation or updates regarding present circumstances. On rare occasions the horseman can personify a horse, a motorcycle or a bicycle.

2- The Clover

Keywords/meanings:
Luck and opportunities knocking at your door is what the clover card communicates. When this picture appears, it is appropriate to take some chances at this point. The clover brings hope and positive outcomes, possibly with a twist of fate. It affects the reading like a joker and can predict unforeseen situations with fortunate vibrations.

Descriptions:
The card describes a high-energy individual, open-minded, who enjoys taking risks in life. For example, gamblers often appear under the clover influence. Excitable, nervous temperaments are the down side of this positive omen. On the negative note, be aware that opportunists and gold diggers are clover types as well.

Astrological reference:
The ruler of the clover is Jupiter (good fortune).
The astrological sign is Sagittarius - fire element - (November 21st to December 21st).
The clover's month is February, (2nd month of the year).

Associated Lenormand playing card:
Six of Diamonds

Special features:
The clover features number 2 on its top side which can be used to estimate a time frame such as February (second month of the year), 2 months, 2 weeks or 2 days.

Body connection:
The card represents the ethereal body or aura.

Card associations:

Clover + horseman (1): good fortune, offers, opportunities, synchronicities

Clover + ship (3): last minute travel, happy trip, a cruise ship

Clover + house (4): happy home, prosperous family

Clover + tree (5): good health, recovery, spiritual protection

Clover + clouds (6): laziness, irresponsibility, gambling addiction

Clover + snake (7): complaisance, trouble-maker, gambler, opportunist

Clover + coffin (8): misfortune, risky situation, negative outcome

Clover + bouquet (9): satisfaction, happiness, positive outcome

Clover + scythe (10): fortunate decisions, leap of faith, calculated risk

Clover + whip (11): sports, competition, winner, successful actions

Clover + birds (12): fortunate discussions, prosperous partnerships, positive talk

Clover + child (13): desired or unexpected pregnancy, happy child

Clover + fox (14): career opportunity, promotion, professional gambler

Clover + bear (15): unforeseen financial windfall, winnings, successful investment

Clover + stars (16): good luck, fortunate synchronicities, unexpected fame

Clover + storks (17): positive changes, improvements

Clover + dog (18): good friendships, helpful people, positive influences

Clover + tower (19): high honours, aristocracy, casino

Clover + garden (20): winnings, casino, race track, lottery, games

Clover + mountain (21): vacation, retreat, mountain resort

Clover + crossroad (22): unexpected opportunity, breakthrough, multiple offers

Clover + mice (23): excitements, anticipation, drug influences, gambling loss

Clover + heart (24): positive relationship, in love, passion, harmony

Clover + ring (25): fertile association, positive alliance, good contract

Clover + book (26): discoveries, revelations, investigation

Clover + letter (27): gift certificate, positive/unexpected news, lottery ticket

Clover + man (28): opportunist, positive thinker, lucky man, upbeat individual

Clover + woman (29): enthusiastic lady, gold digger, risk taker

Clover + lily (30): golden retirement, easy lifestyle

Clover + sun (31): overnight success, outstanding accomplishment

Clover + moon (32): happy moments, romantic situations, sudden fame

Clover + key (33): lucky break, positive twist of fate, lottery winner

Clover + fish (34): prosperous business, increasing sales, business opportunity

Clover + anchor (35): long-term prosperity, stable growth

Clover + cross (36): spiritual or religious contentment, blessings, devotion

Footnotes:
The clover is a lucky card that influences the outcomes of a reading favorably. It is a sign of hope, happy endings and unexpected answers to difficult problems. With this symbol you must think 'outside of the box,' and in a new way, to create surprising and beneficial outcomes. Practice positive thinking toward life.

3- The Ship

Keywords/meanings:
The ship travels far away seeking adventure. Leaving routine and familiar faces behind, it leads to separation, emigration, international travel and transition. With this card you may experience in the future different cultures, countries or weather patterns. Your business may even go through an international growth. Overall this ship leads to exploration and change.

Descriptions:
This vessel brings immigrants and people of foreign descent to you. People under the ship influence are worldly, mobile, and have great life-experience. Sometimes they can be unstable and nomadic, with significant lifestyle differences. All darker skin tones and somber colors are featured under the ship. For example, the symbol often appears to represent an individual of Mediterranean, Asian or African descent, most likely a man.

Astrological reference:
The ruler of the ship is Jupiter (travel).
The astrological sign is Aries - fire element - (March 21st to April 21st).
The ship's month is March, (3rd month of the year).

Associated Lenormand playing card:
Ten of Spades

Special features:
The ship bears the number 3 and you may use this number to estimate a time frame such as March (third month of the year), 3 months, 3 weeks or 3 days.

Body connection:
The symbol is linked with the liver and the gallbladder.

Card associations:

Ship + horseman (1): round trip, back and forth, coming around or coming back

Ship + clover (2): gambling trip, entertaining journey

Ship + house (4): moving away, emigration/immigration, transfer, boat

Ship + tree (5): motion sickness, spiritual journey, rafting

Ship + clouds (6): uncertain voyage, transient, adventure

Ship + snake (7): bumpy ride, car troubles, problems encountered while away

Ship + coffin (8): cancelled vacation/trip, wreckage

Ship + bouquet (9): nice vacation/trip, luxury cruise

Ship + scythe (10): interrupted vacation, accident

Ship + whip (11): off road travel, sportive vacation, bicycle, exhausting trip

Ship + birds (12): passengers, tourists, foreigners, foreign language, plane

Ship + child (13): foreign born child, conception during a trip/vacation

Ship + fox (14): travel/flight/cruise employee, pilot, job with extensive travelling

Ship + bear (15): money transfer, international investment, foreign currency

Ship + stars (16): flying, gliding, skydiving, astronaut, space shuttle, rocket

Ship + storks (17): major changes such as moving, emigration, exile, plane

Ship + dog (18): tourist guide, international friends, travel companion

Ship + tower (19): foreign corporation or government, United Nations

Ship + garden (20): foreign countries, international trips, foreign students

Ship + mountain (21): trip delayed or extended, postponed voyage, exile

Ship + crossroad (22): excursions, tour, road trip, airport, port, train station

Ship + mice (23): difficult transition, stressful trip, mechanical problems

Ship + heart (24): romantic getaway, single cruise, foreign lover

Ship + ring (25): honeymoon, international treaty, green card, overseas wedding

Ship + book (26): archeological research, educational trip, passport

Ship + letter (27): far away news, foreign letter, plane or cruise passes

Ship + man (28): foreigner, airline pilot, captain, importer, traveler

Ship + woman (29): cruise personnel, travel agent, foreign born woman

Ship + lily (30): permanent stay, extended trip, senior vacation, older foreigner

Ship + sun (31): tropical or African destination, desert location, summer vacation

Ship + moon (32): day dreaming, romantic weekends, honeymoon cruise

Ship + key (33): journey of a life time, karmic location, spiritual voyage

Ship + fish (34): import/export business, business trip, transportation, freight

Ship + anchor (35): long travel, transatlantic flight, cruise, island

Ship + cross (36): sentimental voyage, pilgrimage, final voyage

Footnotes:
The ship can impersonate any moving vehicle like cars, motorcycles, boats, planes and others. The card represents a significant distance therefore it may predict a move that is far away to another state or country. At the very least it should mean a change of zip code.

4- The House

Keywords/meanings:
The house is the home that you live in, the family you have created or you are coming from. The card symbolizes all domestic affairs, the intimate life hiding behind closed doors. In addition, it refers to real estate dealings and physical property, like your current address. Small and medium companies, home businesses and family owned enterprises appear through this symbol. The house is a stable card, a sign of refuge and comfort.

Descriptions:
The house brings stable and grounded individuals who may be financially well-off. Their thinking is usually squared and organized, but house people can also be stubborn and overly protective. A house person is very often family oriented with strong traditional values. Men or women under this card tend to feature light or medium brown hair, sometimes ash blonde. Their eyes would be blue, green or hazel, and they may have facial hair.

Astrological reference:
The ruler of the house is the Moon (family).
The astrological sign is Taurus - earth element - (April 21st to May 21st).
The house's month is April (4th month of the year).

Associated Lenormand playing card:
King of Hearts

Special features:
The card connects with the number 4 or the month of April. So the card may estimate a time frame like 4 days, 4 months, etc.

Body connection:
The house is the representation of the human skeleton, the frame of the body.

Card associations:
House + horseman (1): a visit, guest, new family member, new roommate

House + clover (2): home improvements, nice family, positive location

House + ship (3): moving away, emigration, recreation vehicle

House + tree (5): family or house expansion, spiritual family, health center

House + clouds (6): domestic difficulties, negative home environment

House + snake (7): domestic fights, abusive home, house repairs

House + coffin (8): sale or destruction of a house, possible family death

House + bouquet (9): happy home, luxurious estate, interior design

House + scythe (10): sale of a house, domestic separation, family decisions

House + whip (11): domestic violence, gym clubhouse, sex shop, quarrels

House + birds (12): roommates, domestic partners, personal assistant

House + child (13): family, guest house, cottage, childhood house

House + fox (14): construction worker, domestic employee, home robbery

House + bear (15): real estate income, real estate holdings, property manager

House + stars (16): upscale property, celebrity compound, architect

House + storks (17): change of residence, house expansion, moving out

House + dog (18): roommates, pets, assistant living, domestic partner

House + tower (19): real estate trust, large apartment building, penthouse

House + garden (20): large estate, theatre, restaurant, large family

House + mountain (21): long-term resident, ski resort, cabin, remote location

House + crossroad (22): multiple property ownership, real estate transactions

House + mice (23): loss in real estate, house deterioration, stressful home life

House + heart (24): lovely home, loving family

House + ring (25): real estate transaction (purchase, sale or lease)

House + book (26): home office, study, library, bookstore

House + letter (27): property title, real estate contract, escrow

House + man (28): home owner, landlord, stable man

House + woman (29): housewife, landlady, real estate agent

House + lily (30): older property, landmark, antique

House + sun (31): showcase home, energy plant, expensive house

House + moon (32): dream house, designer home, metaphysical shop

House + key (33): first home, spiritual place, entrance, gates

House + fish (34): real estate agency, home based business, home builder

House + anchor (35): family estate, fisherman house, lighthouse, pier

House + cross (36): chapel, memorial, distressed property

Footnotes:

The house is the card to use to find out where you may move to and the circumstances of the relocation. If you would like to analyze the conditions of a house, the situation inside a family or to determine a real estate transaction, you could use this symbol as well. The card may reveal intimate details, sometimes unforeseen problems or bring some reassurance.

5- The Tree

Keywords/meanings:
The tree is the symbol of life and health. It unveils your spiritual believes, your karmic connection to possible soul mates and the vigor of your health. Think about the karmic wheel, the life force, the universe when you look at the tree.

Descriptions:
The person coming with this symbol is usually a spiritual or religious seeker. The individual is centered on a healthy lifestyle, practices spiritual balance and entertains an open mind. All green colors are associated with the tree.

Astrological reference:
The rulers of the tree are the Sun (life force) and the South Lunar Nodes (Karma).
The tree's month is May, (the 5th month of the year).

Associated Lenormand playing card:
Seven of Hearts

Special features:
The tree's number is 5, corresponds to the month of May. Use the number 5 like in 5 days, 5 months, the month of May, or spring time to forecast an event.

Body Connections:
The tree connects with the brain and regulates our mental health.

Card associations:

Tree + horseman (1): health information, spiritual meeting (soul mate)

Tree + clover (2): excellent health, recovery

Tree + ship (3): letting go process, spiritual journey, ambulance

Tree + house (4): stable health, spiritual house, healing center

Tree + clouds (6): unstable health, mental confusion, chemical imbalance

Tree + snake (7): physical problems, illness, ailments, yogi master

Tree + coffin (8): clinical depression, major illness, weak life force

Tree + bouquet (9): good health, positive spiritual connection

Tree + scythe (10): surgery, medical procedure, cut, broken bone, extraction

Tree + whip (11): chronic illness, recurring pains, exercise, post-surgery rehab

Tree + birds (12): soul mates, spiritual couple, spiritual conversations

Tree + child (13): pregnancy, birth, spiritual rebirth, reincarnation

Tree + fox (14): underlying health issues, holistic worker

Tree + bear (15): diet, weight problem, obesity, eating disorder, tumor

Tree + stars (16): medical treatments, psychic, astrologer, laser

Tree + storks (17): birth, recovery, healing

Tree + dog (18): soul mate, physician, holistic expert, psychologist

Tree + tower (19): hospital, clinic, health care facility

Tree + garden (20): healthy, spiritual gathering, garden, Zen environment

Tree + mountain (21): low blood pressure, blockage, fatigue

Tree + crossroad (22): tests, spiritual lessons, self-exploration

Tree + mice (23): health deterioration, anxiety, stress, poor immune system

Tree + heart (24): heart problems, organ donor, karmic love, charity

Tree + ring (25): spiritual connections, karmic relationship, reincarnation cycle

Tree + book (26): health exams, scans, tests, x-rays, karmic lessons

Tree + letter (27): prescriptions, lab results, birth certificate, written will

Tree + man (28): spiritual individual, shaman, soul mate

Tree + woman (29): holistic woman, healer, soul mate, mentally strong

Tree + lily (30): aging problems, senior lifestyle, paralysis, arthritis, dying

Tree + sun (31): strong life force, energetic, survivor, powerful, virility

Tree + moon (32): mental/emotional health, female sex organs, drug influence

Tree + key (33): karmic lessons, soul mate issues, destiny, life purpose

Tree + fish (34): fertility, health care, insurance company, holistic practice

Tree + anchor (35): stable health, long life expectancy, strong immune system

Tree + cross (36): suffering, grief, deep depression, religious belief

Footnotes:
The tree helps to analyze the state of health and answers questions related to soul mate connections. Please note: a 'health reading' should never be used as a substitute for professional medical advice.

6- The Clouds

Keywords/meanings:
The clouds announce temporary confusion, changeable situations and warn against disturbed individuals around you. The symbol makes it harder to give accurate predictions because of its uncertain outcomes. In a reading the clouds bring madness to the mind and instability to the heart. Things have not been revealed as of yet, so prudence is the rule. The picture may unveil abusive relationships, conflicts of interests and deceptions. The clouds feel like a sticky and humid storm, on a hot summer day. Everything is contradictory or mixed. The other characteristic of the clouds is the idea of multiples (duo, duet, twins, yin/yang energies).

Descriptions:
People under the cloud energy are irritable, unstable or unpredictable. They may have bad temperaments, complex personalities or suffer from various mental disorders (bi-polar, Attention Deficit Disorder (ADD), for example). The card can also describe individuals hiding a double-life. The clouds represent all dark and gray colors. Men or women may display hair with highlights or with multiple colors, but the predominant hair coloring is a warm brown. Their eyes are likely to be brown, hazel or blue.

Astrological reference:
The rulers of the clouds are Neptune (illusions) and Mercury (intellect).
The card may also be associated with all air signs which are:
Aquarius (January 21st to February 21st)
Gemini (May 21st to June 21st)
Libra (September 21st to October 21st)
Or in some cases the clouds could connect with the double signs:
Pisces (February 21st to March 21st) and
Libra (September 21st to October 21st)

Note: most often the clouds bring to the reading the influence of the Gemini.

The clouds month is June, (the 6th month of the year).

Associated Lenormand playing card:
King of Clubs

Special features:
The clouds card number is 6, which corresponds to the month of June. This is a possible time frame for an event, which may occur in 6 days, 6 months or during the month of June. The card relates to spring time as well.

Body connection:
The picture sketches the lungs and therefore connects with the respiratory system.

Card associations:
Clouds + horseman (1): clarity, explanation, information on the way

Clouds + clover (2): confusion that works in your favor, bliss, euphoria

Clouds + ship (3): uncertain voyage, air travel, plane

Clouds + house (4): unclear domestic situation, temporary housing, family trouble

Clouds + tree (5): unstable mental health, drug/alcohol abuse, delusions

Clouds + snake (7): serious problems with no easy solutions, vicious circle

Clouds + coffin (8): resolution, relief, reality check

Clouds + bouquet (9): "under the influence" (of drugs, alcohol, medication), bliss

Clouds + scythe (10): irrational decisions, confusion

Clouds + whip (11): threats, harassments, physical fights, abuses

Clouds + birds (12): verbal manipulations, defamation, gossip and lies

Clouds + child (13): capricious child, twins, multiple births, unstable teen

Clouds + fox (14): lies, corruption, misrepresentation, bad employee

Clouds + bear (15): mismanagement, difficult boss, embezzlement, poor diet

Clouds + stars (16): delusions, fantasies, procrastination

Clouds + storks (17): risky move, chaotic change, uncertain progress

Clouds + dog (18): deceptive friends, double-life partner, disloyalty

Clouds + tower (19): lawsuit, mediation, mental institution

Clouds + garden (20): party, happiness, drunk, under the influence

Clouds + mountain (21): dangers, obstacles, delays

Clouds + crossroad (22): confusion, procrastination, indecisive

Clouds + mice (23): anxiety, uncontrollable, doubts, confusion

Clouds + heart (24): infatuation, multiple lovers, promiscuous, affairs

Clouds + ring (25): bad business contract, cheating, resolution

Clouds + book (26): secrets, counterfeiting, investigation, indiscretion

Clouds + letter (27): defamation, tabloids, false advertising, fake papers

Clouds + man (28): con man, confused individual, untrustworthy, unstable

Clouds + woman (29): unstable woman, deceiving individual, Machiavellian

Clouds + lily (30): senior dependants, mental confusion, meditation

Clouds + sun (31): victory, survival, accomplishment

Clouds + moon (32): mood swings, hormonal instability, confusion

Clouds + key (33): insights, signs, solution, revelation

Clouds + fish (34): illegal business, underground activities

Clouds + anchor (35): settling down, mission accomplished, clarity

Clouds + cross (36): sleepless nights, worries, despair

Footnotes:

The clouds make matters more complicated. The symbol does warn against unpredictable outcomes, but most of all it refers back to the idea of "free will." People can change their mind at anytime; they can choose not to follow their feelings and do the opposite of what they truly want. For that reason the clouds are confusing by nature.

The second group of 6 cards is:

    7. The snake: a malicious serpent is waiting in the bushes

    8. The coffin: a hearse on a platform for a last goodbye

    9. The bouquet: a lovely arrangement of flowers to be offered

    10. The scythe: a farmer tool resting near a stack of hay

    11. The whip: instruments of punishment displayed to warn

    12 The birds: two birds as a couple standing on a tree branch

7- The Snake

Keywords/meanings:

The snake predicts difficulties of all sorts: disappointments, jealousy, manipulations and tricks brought on by familiar people. Be aware of your co-workers, your "friends," and even your relatives. The picture is about lies, deceit, defamation, cheating and betrayal. This card is not a good omen regardless of the surrounding cards.

Descriptions:

Very often people who are described by the snake turn out to be users, manipulative, envious and of weak character. They are likely to be verbally or emotionally abusive and they are prone to cheating, lying and stealing. No matter how nice they appear on the outside, you need to be aware of the fact they have a hidden agenda. And they mean trouble! They are your rivals, the other woman or the traitor within your circle of friends. The snake connects with all the green colors. Women could physically look like the archetype of Snow White, long dark hair with fair skin. The eye colors may be either brown or blue.

Astrological reference:

The rulers of the snake are Mars (aggression) and Uranus (unpredictability).
The card may represent two signs both of water element:
Cancer (June 21st to July 21st) and
Scorpio (October 21st to November 21st)
The snake's month is July, (7th month of the year).

Associated Lenormand playing card:

Queen of Clubs

Special features:
The snake's number is 7 symbolizing the month of July: a prediction may occur in 7 days, 7 weeks or during the month of July. The card synchronizes with summer time.

Body connection:
The picture symbolizes the big intestine and the digestive system.

Card associations:
Snake + horseman (1): help is on the way, rescue, solution
Snake + clover (2): helpful opportunity, solution to a problem, repair
Snake + ship (3): difficulties in business, shipping/car troubles, issues on a trip
Snake + house (4): home repairs, domestic troubles, home robbery
Snake + tree (5): contagious illness, sexually transmitted diseases, sickness
Snake + clouds (6): no solution or insight, complete confusion, lost
Snake + coffin (8): end of troubles, resolution, completion
Snake + bouquet (9): positive turn around, repairs, corrections
Snake + scythe (10): surgery, effective solution, cutting off
Snake + whip (11): fights, quarrels, abuses, injuries
Snake + birds (12): negotiations, mediation, compromises
Snake + child (13): troubled teen, challenging child
Snake + fox (14): serious enemies, bad employee, tough job
Snake + bear (15): financial troubles, thief, unscrupulous manager
Snake + stars (16): creative solutions, challenging projects
Snake + storks (17): difficult changes, changes bringing solutions
Snake + dog (18): networking solutions, helping hand, assistance
Snake + tower (19): lawsuit, trial, judgement, court order
Snake + garden (20): wrong social connection, group solutions
Snake + mountain (21): consistent troubles, in a rut
Snake + crossroad (22): escape, running away, avoidance, denial

Snake + mice (23): major incident, bad to worse, destruction, demise

Snake + heart (24): relationship headaches, cheating, deception

Snake + ring (25): compromise, agreement, solution, arrangement

Snake + book (26): troubled past, unpleasant secrets, background check

Snake + letter (27): bad news, sermon, past due invoices, threats

Snake + man (28): abusive individual, trouble maker, in crisis, liar, cheater

Snake + woman (29): manipulative woman, gossip, malicious, spy

Snake + lily (30): letting go, effective solution

Snake + sun (31): difficult victory, costly success

Snake + moon (32): illusions, lies, deception, manipulations

Snake + key (33): effective solution, karmic problems

Snake + fish (34): business troubles, illegal practices

Snake + anchor (35): trust issues, shaky stability

Snake + cross (36): suffering, mental and physical abuse

Footnotes:

The snake is always a warning that "something is up." It may just be minor trouble or indicate more serious issues. Anyone coming under the influence of the snake should be checked very carefully. The snake never fails in uncovering an individual of weak morals and compromised values.

8- The Coffin

Keywords/meanings:
Through major changes in life we test our ability to survive. The coffin could announce negative events such as a serious illness or even a death. But most often, it forecasts important life alterations: starting over or being forced to give up material possessions or a relationship, are common manifestations. The completion of a life cycle like finishing a period of your life (retirement, getting married/ the end of being single) is signified by the picture because of its nature related to spiritual transition. In other words, the coffin means transformation of all sorts. Sometimes the forces of change are negative, but in some instances, they can be liberating and therefore positive. Destructive behaviors and negative attitudes may be present in someone's life when this card appears.

Descriptions:
Depressed, negative, sick individuals usually come through this symbol. These people are bad omen because their issues have the potential to overwhelm one's life to the point of destruction. They carry a feeling of a "black cloud" over them, and can be emotional vampires. The coffin associates with any shade of blacks or deep dark colors.

Astrological reference:
The ruler of the coffin is Pluto (transformation).
The astrological sign is Leo - fire element - (July 21st to August 21st).
The coffin's month is August, (8th month of the year).

Associated Lenormand playing card:
Nine of Diamonds

Special features:
This card with the number 8 could predict an event happening in August or during the Leo time. It can also refer to a time cycle like 8 days, 8 weeks and so on. The coffin is a summer card.

Body connection:
The picture connects with the last part of our intestines and the anus.

Card associations:
Coffin + horseman (1): new beginnings, a new cycle in life, renewal

Coffin + clover (2): rebirth, a second chance, new start in life

Coffin + ship (3): exile, running away, emigration, in rare instances death

Coffin + house (4): reconstruction, rebuilding, redoing, new foundations

Coffin + tree (5): serious illness, clinical depression, weak health

Coffin + clouds (6): mental confusion, nervous breakdown, depression

Coffin + snake (7): major hardships, disputed probate

Coffin + bouquet (9): recovery, rebound, funeral, memorial

Coffin + scythe (10): accident, self-inflicted difficulties, sacrifice, self-mutilation

Coffin + whip (11): war, beating, mutilation, destructive behaviours

Coffin + birds (12): depressive news, news of a death

Coffin + child (13): destructive youngster, depressed teen

Coffin + fox (14): depressing work, coroner office employee, funeral employment

Coffin + bear (15): inheritance, funeral expenses, trust, life insurance proceeds

Coffin + stars (16): positive transition, liberation, relief, rescue, fresh start

Coffin + storks (17): forced changes, letting go, moving on

Coffin + dog (18): friend in need, emotional vampire, grief therapist

Coffin + tower (19): morgue, hospice, prison

Coffin + garden (20): cemetery, funeral gathering, support system

Coffin + mountain (21): desperate longing, stuck, isolation, agony

Coffin + crossroad (22): separation, new life direction, transition

Coffin + mice (23): suicidal, depression, phobias, mental illness

Coffin + heart (24): grief, emotional healing, forgiveness, trauma

Coffin + ring (25): repairs, recovery, completion, starting over

Coffin + book (26): death investigation, autopsy, archeology, history

Coffin + letter (27): death announcement, will, resignation

Coffin + man (28): depressed individual, suicidal, in crisis, dying

Coffin + woman (29): mentally down, negative thinker, in shock, traumatized

Coffin + lily (30): old age, antique, dying, assisted living

Coffin + sun (31): rebirth, resuscitation, victory, survivor

Coffin + moon (32): emotional despair, spiritual depression, shock

Coffin + key (33): karma, spiritual transformation

Coffin + fish (34): mortician, funeral business

Coffin + anchor (35): agony, extended life, longing

Coffin + cross (36): suicidal thoughts, pains, sadness, grief

Footnotes:
Do not be fearful of the coffin. Instead think of big changes, life transitions, and new cycles. But if you ask a simple yes/no question, then the answer is "no or never." Be aware that the coffin often appears around people who are depressed or physically down. The card is rarely a warning of death!

9- The Bouquet

Keywords/meanings:
The bouquet is beauty, grace and joy. The picture forecasts happy times, recovery of any kind, wellness and granted wishes. It is a gift, a thank you to enjoy. The positive vibrations of the card are very strong. With it, you know you are welcome and appreciated. The bouquet is a big smile to warm your heart as it is the card of spiritual and emotional healing.

Descriptions:
The card represents charming and smiling people. It personifies grace, beauty and warmth. Physically a "bouquet" person usually displays beautiful hair, a photogenic face and a perfect smile. Women may be exotic looking, or model types. The picture may refer to individuals who are emotionally available or newly single. All colors of the rainbow are also part of the bouquet.

Astrological reference:
The ruler of the bouquet is Venus (beauty).
The astrological sign is Virgo - earth element - (August 21st to September 21st).
The bouquet's month is September, (9th month of the year).

Associated Lenormand playing card:
Queen of Spades

Special features:
September and the Virgo cycle are possible timetables. You can also use 9 for 9 days, 9 weeks, etc.

Body connection:
The symbol is linked with the face, the smile and the hair.

Card associations:

Bouquet + horseman (1): new people coming into your life, happy encounter

Bouquet + clover (2): happiness, good fortune

Bouquet + ship (3): vacation, cruise, boat, luxury vehicle

Bouquet + house (4): lovely neighborhood, domestic harmony, attractive home

Bouquet + tree (5): good health, physical harmony, spiritual balance

Bouquet + clouds (6): stagnation, laziness, procrastination, dream state

Bouquet + snake (7): jealous, envious, superficial, capricious

Bouquet + coffin (8): disappointments, drama, ending

Bouquet + scythe (10): cosmetic surgery, haircut, positive decisions

Bouquet + whip (11): gym, yoga, dancing, harmonious sexuality

Bouquet + birds (12): good conversations, gatherings, meetings

Bouquet + child (13): lovely kid, attractive teen

Bouquet + fox (14): job in cosmetic, fashion or design industries

Bouquet + bear (15): positive cash flow, performing investments

Bouquet + stars (16): up and coming, achievement, hopes and dreams

Bouquet + storks (17): growth, positive changes, progress

Bouquet + dog (18): great friends, pleasant partner, harmonious friendships

Bouquet + tower (19): entertainment venue (theatre, casino, amusement park)

Bouquet + garden (20): crowd, audience, recreational area

Bouquet + mountain (21): peace, restful, outdoor park, nature

Bouquet + crossroad (22): opportunities, hiking, nature walks

Bouquet + mice (23): short term joy, anticipation, excitements

Bouquet + heart (24): romantic happiness, handsome lover, love

Bouquet + ring (25): happy marriage, enjoyable partnership

Bouquet + book (26): positive discoveries, design project, flora studies

Bouquet + letter (27): happy news, invitations, stationary

Bouquet + man (28): attractive man, model, gentleman, handsome

Bouquet + woman (29): beautiful woman, lovely, charming, happy

Bouquet + lily (30): serenity, harmony, enjoyable retirement

Bouquet + sun (31): honorable victory, outstanding achievement, celebration

Bouquet + moon (32): emotional happiness, satisfaction, contentment

Bouquet + key (33): outstanding beauty, incredible success

Bouquet + fish (34): female consumer, beauty industry, modeling

Bouquet + anchor (35): long lasting happiness, stable/harmonious life

Bouquet + cross (36): generosity, philanthropy, charitable

Footnotes:

The beautiful bouquet is happy, frivolous and light hearted. It is the "yes" card for most simple questions and a positive sign in readings.

10- The Scythe

Keywords/meanings:
The scythe is the decision maker cutting into circumstances without hesitation. It brings shockwaves and accidents of all sorts. The picture may predict emotional separations, love rejections or violent acts perpetrated by others. One may take hurtful actions against another. The scythe's effects are usually final or irreversible. The symbol may personify the instrument of the surgeon, the scalpel. Therefore the card could forecast a surgery. Nevertheless, the aftermath of the scythe's path may be positive (harvest) or negative (cutting off).

Descriptions:
People under the scythe's influence are sharp, quick and analytical. Their temperament can be cold and hurtful at times. They can make executive decisions at critical moments and demonstrate leadership qualities. Surgeons often appear through this symbol.

Astrological reference:
The ruler of the scythe is Mars (action).
The astrological sign is Libra - air element - (September 21st to October 21st).
The scythe's month is October (10th month of the year).

Associated Lenormand playing card:
Jack of diamonds

Special features:
The Libra cycle and October are possible time references to find out when a situation is most likely to take place. The scythe synchronizes with the fall season.

Body connection:
The scythe is a sharp instrument and as such it relates to the teeth and mouth.

Card associations:

Scythe + horseman (1): cutting off the old to welcome the new, opening up

Scythe + clover (2): good decisions, positive outcomes

Scythe + ship (3): leaving, emigrating, sudden separation, running away

Scythe + house (4): purchase or sale of a house, family decisions

Scythe + tree (5): surgery, medical instrument, biopsy, extraction

Scythe + clouds (6): uncertain outcome, weak decisions, indecisive

Scythe + snake (7): nuisance, attack, painful decision

Scythe + coffin (8): destruction, termination, resignation, giving up

Scythe + bouquet (9): positive outcome, smart decisions, sculpture, crafts

Scythe + whip (11): violence, rape, fight, weapon, knife

Scythe + birds (12): arguments, militants, soldiers, dissidents

Scythe + child (13): abortion, miscarriage, in uterus surgery, caesarean

Scythe + fox (14): resignation, lay off, carpenter, butcher

Scythe + bear (15): investment decisions, weight loss surgery

Scythe + stars (16): plan, strategy for action, new life direction

Scythe + storks (17): initiatives for a change, moving on, proactive

Scythe + dog (18): brutal separation, letting go of someone

Scythe + tower (19): emergency room, hospital, trial, judgment

Scythe + garden (20): jurors, critics, sowing, gardening, harvesting

Scythe + mountain (21): withdraw, slow procedure, not done yet, stalling

Scythe + crossroad (22): separation, separate lives, decision to make

Scythe + mice (23): breaking down, stressful/ineffective decision

Scythe + heart (24): break up, hurtful relationship, heart surgery

Scythe + ring (25): legal separation, annulment, broken commitment

Scythe + book (26): researcher, autopsy, analysis, restoration
Scythe + letter (27): request, notice of action, divorce papers
Scythe + man (28): critical individual, sharp, hurtful
Scythe + woman (29): decisive person, surgeon, leader
Scythe + lily (30): healing, scars, rebuilding, renovation
Scythe + sun (31): assertive, victory, strong leadership
Scythe + moon (32): release, emotional decision, break up
Scythe + key (33): significant decision, karmic lessons, fate
Scythe + fish (34): business decisions, executives, weapon
  manufacturer
Scythe + anchor (35): irreversible decision, long-term strategy
Scythe + cross (36): injury, self inflected wound, sacrifice

Footnotes:
The scythe informs you of possible surgery when dealing with health questions. It also warns against unexpected repairs concerning your household appliances, plumbing system or your car. If someone makes a decision under this symbol then it is likely to be irreversible.

11- The Whip

Keywords/meanings:
This picture announces arguments, fights that may lead to divorce or separation. The violence of this card could lead to abuses, tortures and suffering. The whip is the sexual card (the phallus) and is an indicator for sexual chemistry and passion. But the symbol can get twisted and therefore represents any kind of deviances and addictions. The whip connects with sports or any physical activity.

Descriptions:
The whip often portrays individuals who are sexy, attractive and seductive. They are likely to be well-endowed and they do understand their sexual power. The negative aspect is that the person with the whip may be a possible violent, addicted or tormented individual posing danger to others. Some whip people can become stalkers, co-dependent in relationships or drug or/ and alcohol addicts. On a positive note, the whip may also refer to athletes, active personalities, and competitive individuals.

Astrological reference:
The rulers of the whip are Mars (sex) and Pluto (deviance).
The astrological sign is Scorpio - water element - (October 21st to November 21st).
The whip's month is November (the 11th month of the year).

Associated Lenormand playing card:
Jack of Clubs

Special features:
The Scorpio period and the month of November can be used to estimate when an event may take place. The winter season can also be interpreted as a time frame.

Body connection:
The whip has a phallus connection, but also refers to our muscles and tendons.

Card associations:
Whip + horseman (1): retaliation, revenge, counter attack, feedback
Whip + clover (2): physical activities, sports, effective actions
Whip + ship (3): globetrotter, explorer, speed boat
Whip + house (4): domestic abuses, personal gym, sexual activity
Whip + tree (5): chronic health problems, tantric sex, stimulation
Whip + clouds (6): going in circles, lack of direction, addictions
Whip + snake (7): troublemaker, dangerous acquaintance, danger
Whip + coffin (8): killing, destruction, physical danger
Whip + bouquet (9): enjoyable sexual life, physical exercises, dancing
Whip + scythe (10): restrained, cancelled, terminated, accident
Whip + birds (12): verbal abuses, arguments, passionate conversation, debate
Whip + child (13): hyper-active child, athletic kid, competitive teen
Whip + fox (14): physically demanding job, fast pace work environment
Whip + bear (15): body builder, athlete, residual income
Whip + stars (16): apprentice, groupie, coaching
Whip + storks (17): fast pace changes, quick progress
Whip + dog (18): stalker, sexual partner, trainer, competitor
Whip + tower (19): army, military base, fortress, stadium
Whip + garden (20): classroom, students, attendees, workshops
Whip + mountain (21): restrictions, limitations, confinement, impasse
Whip + crossroad (22): hyperactivity, busy, unsettled, roaming
Whip + mice (23): stressful physical activity, exhaustion, obsessions
Whip + heart (24): sexual satisfaction, passionate relationship

Whip + ring (25): co-dependency, addictions, marital abuse
Whip + book (26): contest, exam, learning, reading
Whip + letter (27): erotic communication, sexually explicit materials, threats
Whip + man (28): attractive male, sexy, physically fit
Whip + woman (29): sexy woman, seductive, intense
Whip + lily (30): chronic ailments due to aging, arthritis, fatigue
Whip + sun (31): virility, sexual charisma, predator, winner
Whip + moon (32): obsessive compulsive, sexual contentment, in lust
Whip + key (33): final act, decisive action, karmic relationship
Whip + fish (34): physical therapist, chiropractor, personal trainer
Whip + anchor (35): regularity, schedule, dependable, consistent
Whip + cross (36): whining, needy, crying, karmic lessons

Footnotes:
The whip is a fast acting card affecting the mind and the heart. Sexual chemistry and physical attraction happen under its influence sometimes overruling our best judgment. The symbol appears when someone suffers an addiction or if the individual may be potentially violent. People split when the whip shows up because it brings arguments and differences. This is a powerful picture to see in a relationship reading.

12- The Birds

Keywords/meanings:
The birds are full of conversation and information: verbal exchanges, phone calls, meetings are to be expected. The picture rules sales, negotiations and public relations. When you do a speech, attend a group session or have an interview, the birds will appear. The symbol connects with couples as well as it does predict dates, companionship or personal connections. Twins, siblings, small group gatherings relate to the birds.

Descriptions:
Individuals identifying with the birds card are social, communicative and curious. Good sales professionals, lawyers, mediators are represented through this card. The birds may reveal media careers, communication talents. The picture portrays friendly and open minded individuals with much to say.

Astrological reference:
The ruler of the birds is Mercury (communication).
The astrological signs are Sagittarius - fire element - (November 21st to December 21st) and Capricorn - earth element - (December 21st to January 21st).
The birds' month is December (12th month of the year).

Associated Lenormand playing card:
Seven of Diamonds

Special features:
The card's number 12 may indicate either the month of December or the Sagittarius/Capricorn cycle as a timetable for future events. It is also a winter card.

Body connection:
The birds of communication symbolize the vocal cords and the throat.

Card associations:
Birds + horseman (1): comments, feedbacks, response, interview
Birds + clover (2): productive meeting, lucky encounters, motivation speech
Birds + ship (3): foreign language, foreign companion, travelers, airplane
Birds + house (4): roommates, living companion, fraternity house
Birds + tree (5): spiritual connection, soul mate, meaningful conversation
Birds + clouds (6): miscommunication, misleading information, small talk
Birds + snake (7): defamation, gossips, difficult negotiation, disagreement
Birds + coffin (8): rupture in communication, end of a relationship
Birds + bouquet (9): pleasant conversation, lovely meeting, fun group
Birds + scythe (10): interrupted negotiation, rupture, collegial decision
Birds + whip (11): arguments, difference of opinions, sport buddies
Birds + child (13): twins, siblings, playmates
Birds + fox (14): sales person, lawyer, airline employee, colleagues
Birds + bear (15): financial consultant, group leader, traffic controller
Birds + stars (16): support group, fans, astronauts, pilots
Birds + storks (17): merger, couple's life, flying, graduation
Birds + dog (18): best friends, companions, siblings, relatives
Birds + tower (19): court of law, senate, congress
Birds + garden (20): workshops, attendees, passengers, audience
Birds + mountain (21): unresponsive, silent

Birds + crossroad (22): separation, twins, siblings

Birds + mice (23): annoying conversation, incoherent, negative talk

Birds + heart (24): romantic partners, emotional conversation

Birds + ring (25): engagement, spouse, agreement

Birds + book (26): mentor, students, seminars, classes

Birds + letter (27): news media, emails, internet, press conference

Birds + man (28): excellent communicator, negotiator, in a relationship

Birds + woman (29): girlfriend, good communicator, pilot

Birds + lily (30): seniors, experienced consultant, serious discussions

Birds + sun (31): successful meeting, positive agreement

Birds + moon (32): acting, singing, stage performance, movie

Birds + key (33): public announcement, karmic partnership, soul mate

Birds + fish (34): sales, shipping, boat, airline

Birds + anchor (35): long-term relationship, life partner

Birds + cross (36): prayers, choir, congregation

Footnotes:

The birds describe the level of communication skill between two people. The card can unveil the nature of a relationship and the future possibilities.

The third group of 6 cards is:

13. The child: a healthy child full of life and energy

14. The fox: a red fox hiding behind a bush until danger passes

15. The bear: a huge grizzly bear looking for food and shelter

16. The stars: a clear starling night without the moon

17. The storks: a couple of storks make their nest on a chimney top

18 The dog: an affectionate mutt waiting for the master's return

13- The Child

Keywords/meanings:
The child reminds us of our childhood, our teenage years and our innocence. It symbolizes fragility, sincerity, immaturity and the eternal youth. We care for what is small and cute, our offspring. With this card, think tiny!

Descriptions:
The picture defines most of the time small framed (petite) or shorter than average individuals. Youthful people with sincere and lively spontaneous temperaments are child like. In a negative way, they can be capricious, immature or irresponsible. Mentally challenged individuals are part of the meaning as well. The card usually refers to a baby, a child or a teen.

Astrological reference:
The ruler of the child is the Moon (childhood).

Associated Lenormand playing card:
Jack of Spades

Special features:
The child may forecast a pregnancy. You can determine the sex of the baby by looking at the immediate cards surrounding it. For example, a masculine card will tend to indicate a son. You could mentally associate the first name of a child or teen with this card to reveal their life's path and current issues during a reading.

Body connection:
The child relates to the chest and the breasts.

Card associations:

Child + horseman (1): birth announcement, pregnancy confirmation

Child + clover (2): gifted child, happy kid, talented teen

Child + ship (3): small trip, foreign adoption, foster child, small car or boat

Child + house (4): guest house, cottage, daycare, babysitting

Child + tree (5): pregnancy, birth, fertility

Child + clouds (6): twins, siblings, multiple births

Child + snake (7): trouble maker, unruly, difficult child

Child + coffin (8): miscarriage, sterility, childless, loss of a child

Child + bouquet (9): cute kid, lovely child, happy teen

Child + scythe (10): abortion, surgery on a child, knife, delivery

Child + whip (11): aggressive kid, bully, overactive child

Child + birds (12): siblings, group of kids, playmates

Child + fox (14): youth work, job involving kids, student job

Child + bear (15): robust kid, overweight child

Child + stars (16): excellent student, gifted kid, child star

Child + storks (17): pregnancy, birth, growth

Child + dog (18): playmate, childhood friend, young friend

Child + tower (19): teenager, high school, board of education

Child + garden (20): students, day care, child playground

Child + mountain (21): disability, slow growth, autism, lonely kid

Child + crossroad (22): twins, siblings, multiple births, day trips

Child + mice (23): viruses, germs, sick kid, needy

Child + heart (24): spontaneous child, loving kid, teenage love

Child + ring (25): legitimate child, heir, adoption, small contract

Child + book (26): genealogy, school, home work

Child + letter (27): birth records, pictures, birth announcement

Child + man (28): short individual, teenager, boy, immature male

Child + woman (29): petite woman, teenager, girl, doll like

Child + lily (30): immature adult, youthful looking, early retirement, oldest kid

Child + sun (31): successful child, competitive teen, energetic kid

Child + moon (32): creative child, artistic teen, psychic youngster

Child + key (33): karmic child, spiritual kid

Child + fish (34): fertility, business geared toward kids, adoption agency

Child + anchor (35): reliable kid, responsible teen

Child + cross (36): abandonment issues, childhood pains, depressed teen

Footnotes:

The child can reveal a pregnancy or the number of children you may have by looking at the surrounding cards (the numbers on top). It can be used to represent a young child or teen in a reading.

14- The Fox

Keywords/meanings:
The fox is work in general like our daily job, our career, our employment. But the card could also reveal deceit, lies and manipulation. The picture foretells the possibility of traps and disloyalty among "friends" or coming from new acquaintances. Prudence in all actions and words is advisable. Learning to trust one's instincts can help avoid such unpleasantness. Discretion is the key.

Descriptions:
The symbol reveals the bad influences of certain individuals surrounding us. Sneaky, cunning personalities as well as liars and spies are part of the negative side of the fox card. On the positive note the animal can portray street smarts and workaholics. Typically the fox profiles an employee, working a 9 to 5 job. The physical aspect of the animal gives short limbs, short noses, reddish tone hair colors and freckles. All red, auburn, copper colors are represented.

Astrological reference:
The ruler of the fox is Neptune (delusions).

Associated Lenormand playing card:
Nine of Clubs

Special features:
The fox can indicate what kind of job or career someone does in observing the cards surrounding the symbol. Remember that the fox usually applies to a job while the fish card talks about a business.

Body connection:
The fox deals with the nose and the scent.

Card associations:

Fox + horseman (1): new employee, new recruit, new job opportunity

Fox + clover (2): career opportunity, promotion, reward

Fox + ship (3): travel for professional reasons, job in tourism, job on a cruise ship

Fox + house (4): domestic employee, personal assistant, deceitful family member

Fox + tree (5): healthcare specialist, health industry employee, holistic work

Fox + clouds (6): cunning individual, deceitful employee

Fox + snake (7): liar, robber, dangerous job, illegal work

Fox + coffin (8): end of contract, lay off, resignation, unemployment

Fox + bouquet (9): beauty expert, cosmetic industry employee, hair dresser

Fox + scythe (10): resignation, quitting, accident on the job

Fox + whip (11): physical therapist, gym employee, abusive worker

Fox + birds (12): telemarketing professional, sales employee, representative

Fox + child (13): childcare provider, school employee, nanny

Fox + bear (15): bank teller, restaurant employee, manager

Fox + star (16): upper management, coach, aerospace employee, pilot

Fox + stork (17): promotion, change of job

Fox + dog (18): personal/medical assistant, consultant

Fox + tower (19): administrative employee (bank, government, corporation)

Fox + garden (20): retail professional, movie theater employee, park employee

Fox + mountain (21): job freeze, stalling career, unemployment, leave of absence

Fox + crossroad (22): job openings, interviews, multiple job offers, part-time jobs

Fox + mice (23): job loss, work reorganization, stressful job

Fox + heart (24): enjoyable job, passion in a career, vocation

Fox + ring (25): employment contract, top employee, union

Fox + book (26): accountant, book keeper, librarian, detective

Fox + letter (27): licensed professional, work certification, diploma

Fox + man (28): employed, hard worker, cunning individual, scam artist

Fox + woman (29): indiscreet, disloyal, liar, deceptive woman

Fox + lily (30): work experience, established career, elderly worker

Fox + sun (31): professional reputation, ambition, valued employee

Fox + moon (32): spiritual or psychological counselor, psychic, artist

Fox + key (33): important job position, key employee, expert

Fox + fish (34): trader, import/export employee, oceanographer

Fox + anchor (35): job seniority, long-term employee, seaport employee

Fox + cross (36): priest, charity worker, rescue worker

Footnotes:

The fox card describes all kinds of con artists. Detectives and law enforcement employees are also represented as they have to be sneaky and creative to catch the bad guys. But, be mindful that the symbol can be a warning signaling a disloyal individual.

15- The Bear

Keywords/meanings:
The bear brings cash flow and financial windfalls. The animal deals with all financial matters regarding your personal finances such as investments, checks or your business life, like account payables and receivables. The picture talks about the top management in a company, the corporate executive or the boss. Its power is physical, but also protective. Sometimes it refers to politics, government personalities and executive branches. Finally, the bear connects with health matters through nutrition, diet and weight control.

Descriptions:
The "bear" person is strong, muscled with usually a large torso or an over-developed upper body. Big people with overweight issues (sweet tooth) will fall into the physical profile. But think also of bodybuilders, athletes who work their bodies as an art form.
Psychologically an individual under the influence of this symbol could be possessive, protective, nurturing, excessively controlling, or overbearing. The card could describe a politician, a financial consultant or a millionaire. On a funny note, bear people are usually very hairy!

Astrological reference:
The ruler of the bear is Jupiter (protection).
The astrological sign is Taurus - earth element - (April 21st to May 21st).

Associated Lenormand playing card:
Ten of Clubs

Special features:
Masculine by nature, the bear rarely associates itself with a woman unless she works in a specific industry like finance, nutrition, or physical training.

Body connection:
The bear is the stomach part of the digestive system.

Card associations:
Bear + horseman (1): new source of income, improved cash flow
Bear + clover (2): financial gains through lucky circumstances, prosperity
Bear + ship (3): money transfer, international investment, expensive trip
Bear + house (4): real estate equity, bed and breakfast, cozy home
Bear + tree (5): nutrition, diet, exercises, food
Bear + clouds (6): financial mismanagement, money laundering
Bear + snake (7): debts, financial difficulties, overpowered
Bear + coffin (8): bankruptcy, investment loss, starvation
Bear + bouquet (9): good financial life, prosperity, body sculpting
Bear + scythe (10): financial decisions, investment transaction, closing accounts
Bear + whip (11): recurring financial problems, physical exercises, body building
Bear + birds (12): financial negotiations, stock market, volatile investments
Bear + child (13): overweight child, strong kid, small savings
Bear + fox (14): financial advisor, gym employee, manager
Bear + star (16): financial portfolio, financial bonus, chef
Bear + storks (17): capital gains, financial improvements
Bear + dog (18): trader, financial advisor, nutritionist
Bear + tower (19): bank, white house, treasury department
Bear + garden (20): financial prosperity, mutual funds, restaurant
Bear + mountain (21): lack of income, financial struggle
Bear + crossroad (22): diversification, multiple sources of income
Bear + mice (23): financial losses, financial mistakes
Bear + heart (24): financial generosity, donations, charity
Bear + ring (25): transaction, financial agreement, life insurance

Bear + book (26): financial industry, accounting, audit, financial analysis

Bear + letter (27): check, invoice, bills, cash

Bear + man (28): body builder, obese individual, financial advisor, strong

Bear + woman (29): overweight woman, caring individual, powerful female

Bear + lily (30): bonds, life insurance annuities, nest egg, pension plan

Bear + sun (31): financial success, prosperity, millionaire

Bear + moon (32): financial instability, creative cash flow, royalties

Bear + key (33): financial breakthrough, financial reward

Bear + fish (34): financial business, mortgage company, loan officer

Bear + anchor (35): financial stability, long-term financial goals, planning

Bear + cross (36): charitable donations, non-profit organization, ministry

Footnotes:

The bear card is essential to assess the financial health of an individual or a company. Forecasting financial fluctuations in a business relies on the bear and its surrounding cards. For health matters, the symbol describes the food intakes and nutritional habits of a person. It may indicate obesity and food allergies. Sometimes the bear warns against the possibility of cancer cells - cysts in the body - so if you get a "bad feeling" about a health inquiry, please refer your client to their regular physician.

16- The Stars

Keywords/meanings:
The stars guide humans to their destiny. They show the way to our dreams for the future. The picture brings up our imagination, our ideals, our hopes and our visions. The star also forecasts fame and reputation that one may be blessed with. The symbol announces new steps, a new path in life, a healing or an encouragement.

Descriptions:
The individual next to the stars can be well known, famous, and recognizable in his or her field. Cheerful and inspirational the "star" person leads by being a role model, a mentor to others, a teacher. Such a person may display attributes of innovation, genius mind or idealistic tendencies. Sometimes a dreamer he or she could be living a life of sand castles and delusions, but with an optimistic attitude.

Astrological reference:
The ruler of the stars is Jupiter (good fortune).
The astrological sign is Aquarius - air element - (January 21st to February 21st).

Associated Lenormand playing card:
Six of Hearts

Special features:
The stars like the tarot card of the same name connect with the zodiac sign Aquarius. Night time could be a time reference on when an event may occur.

Body connection:
The stars are the human skin.

Card associations:

Star + horseman (1): hopes being fulfilled, answers to prayers, great news

Star + clover (2): lucky break, good fortune, happy circumstances

Star + ship (3): international reputation, space travel, rocket

Star + house (4): architect, interior designer, dream house

Star + tree (5): healer, holistic practices, spiritual lifestyle, guru

Star + clouds (6): confusion, indecision, lack of life direction

Star + snake (7): corruption, difficulties to reach goals, challenging path

Star + coffin (8): giving up, surrender, depression, disillusions

Star + bouquet (9): healthy ambitions, celebrity, fame, top model

Star + scythe (10): execution, implementation, inspired action

Star + whip (11): training, discipline, professional athlete, winner

Star + birds (12): public speaker, top sales person, spoke person

Star + child (13): gifted, genius, child actor, young celebrity

Star + fox (14): key employee, promotion, aerospace employee, casting agent

Star + bear (15): financial goals, investment strategies, financial planning

Star + storks (17): aspiration, upgrades, positive changes

Star + dog (18): notoriety, celebrity, reputable therapist, celebrity assistant

Star + tower (19): corporate ladder, high ambitions, General, President

Star + garden (20): award ceremony, gala, public event, celebration

Star + mountain (21): late bloomer, slow progress, dream on hold

Star + crossroad (22): versatile abilities, multiple achievements

Star + mice (23): stage fright, demise, demotion, loss of reputation

Star + heart (24): philanthropist, humanitarian, popular, favorite

Star + ring (25): accomplishment, honor, nomination

Star + book (26): inspired teachings, successful writer, best seller

Star + letter (27): headlines, announcement, awards, recommendation

Star + man (28): idealistic individual, famous, architect, engineer

Star + woman (29): mentor, inspirational, popular woman, positive

Star + lily (30): retirement, golden years, older celebrity, retired star

Star + sun (31): stardom, leading personality, champion, outstanding individual

Star + moon (32): fame, creative genius, famous psychic, astrologer

Star + key (33): winner, awards, medals, trophy

Star + fish (34): aerospace, engineering, architecture, casting

Star + anchor (35): legendary, legacy, hall of fame

Star + cross (36): religious leader, religious dogma

Footnotes:

The stars predict positive outcomes with some form of recognition coming from others. It is an encouraging sign to any difficult question and reinforces the pursuit of your dreams. Success is within your reach!

17- The Storks

Keywords/meanings:
The storks mean changes in your home like moving or the birth of a child. Mainly an improvement card talking about transition and evolution, the symbol brings novelties that were not expected and family additions of all sorts like adoption, mother-in-law, etc.

Descriptions:
The card describes an elegant person, likely tall with long limbs and a long nose. Personality wise, the storks show adaptability, flexibility and a practical side. The "stork" person is usually positive and refined. On the other hand the storks may announce a pregnancy if the "woman" card stands next to it. Women under the influence of the storks tend to be blonde or dark blonde with light color of eyes.

Astrological reference:
The rulers of the storks are Jupiter (travel) and Uranus (changes).

Associated Lenormand playing card:
Queen of Hearts

Special features:
The card refers to seasonal changes like spring time. These indicators are useful to estimate when an event is supposed to take place.

Body connection:
The storks are the legs.

Card associations:

Storks + horseman (1): back and forth, addition to the family unit

Storks + clover (2): positive move, changes bringing luck

Storks + ship (3): moving away, emigration, visa changes

Storks + house (4): moving or remodeling, new family member

Storks + tree (5): recovery from illness, empowerment, getting better

Storks + clouds (6): uncertainty about the future, irrational changes

Storks + snake (7): obstacles against progress, challenges to overcome

Storks + coffin (8): cancellation, annulment, reconsideration

Storks + bouquet (9): positive changes, improvements

Storks + scythe (10): definitive changes, end of a cycle

Storks + whip (11): going around in circles, training, gymnastic athlete

Storks + birds (12): progress in relationship, improved intimacy, mediation

Storks + child (13): birth or pregnancy

Storks + fox (14): positive job change, promotion

Storks + bear (15): financial gains, stock trading, higher income

Storks + stars (16): projects, future plans, moving forward

Storks + dog (18): good friendships, stimulating friends, coach

Storks + tower (19): building, moving up

Storks + garden (20): positive changes, increased popularity

Storks + mountain (21): temporary setback, slow progress

Storks + crossroad (22): expansion, diversification, separation

Storks + mice (23): discouragement, disappointments, waste of efforts

Storks + heart (24): good intentions, next step in a relationship

Storks + ring (25): commitment, marriage, engagement, promises

Storks + book (26): advance studies, researcher, high tech industry

Storks + letter (27): proposal, submission, recommendation letter

Storks + man (28): flexible individual, progressive, moving forward

Storks + woman (29): elegant woman, up and coming individual
Storks + lily (30): experience, maturity, reaching retirement
Storks + sun (31): achievements, success, victory
Storks + moon (32): emotional satisfaction, artistic excellence
Storks + key (33): benchmark, twist of fate, life changing event
Storks + fish (34): profitable enterprise, business success, airlines
Storks + anchor (35): long-term effects, stable progress
Storks + cross (36): painful changes, reluctant progress

Footnotes:
The storks could announce a pregnancy if there is a repetition of fertility signs that point in that direction. Most likely in a reading the card will appear to show improvements or changes in your personal life.

18- The Dog

Keywords/meanings:

The dog is a friend, a person you can trust. It usually refers to someone you know quite well or someone you just met once. The card adds reliability, closeness and faithfulness in love relationships. Linked with intimacy and habits, the dog tells you that you can trust this connection. This symbol is the life companion you have been longing for.

Descriptions:

A "dog" person is friendly, loving and stable. The dog is faithful and dependable. Under its vibrations, people listen and respond with compassion and willingness. All brown colors are represented.

Astrological reference:

The ruler of the dog is Venus (love).

Associated Lenormand playing card:

Ten of Hearts

Special features:

When this card appears in a spread it may foresee a soul mate coming to meet you at this point of time. If not, the dog talks of a person already known by the inquirer. Either way this person is no stranger.

Body connection:

The dog refers to the tongue and the taste.

Card associations:

Dog + horseman (1): new friendships, new companionship

Dog + clover (2): help from a friend, prosperous friends

Dog + ship (3): foreign friendships, travel companion

Dog + house (4): family friend, pet, live-in companion, housekeeper

Dog + tree (5): doctors, psychologists, nurses, soul mates

Dog + clouds (6): deficient relationship, superficial friend

Dog + snake (7): betrayal, difficult friendship, pretense

Dog + coffin (8): rupture, end of relationship, death of a friend

Dog + bouquet (9): nice friendships, attractive companion, lovely friends

Dog + scythe (10): break up, accident around someone you know

Dog + whip (11): co-dependents, trainer or training partners, abusive companion

Dog + birds (12): Conversations, parties, get together, reunion

Dog + child (13): playmates, puppy, school mates

Dog + fox (14): disloyalty, rescuers, medical assistant

Dog + bear (15): advisors, consultant, security guard

Dog + stars (16): famous friends, cast, entourage

Dog + storks (17): "more than friends," supportive friends

Dog + tower (19): friends in high places, jail mates, experts, specialists

Dog + garden (20): acquaintances, networks, clubs, organizations

Dog + mountain (21): rejection, alienation, indifference from someone you know

Dog + crossroad (22): many friends, superficial social life, short term friendships

Dog + mice (23): friendship in peril, stressful relationships

Dog + heart (24): emotional buddy, love companion

Dog + ring (25): loyalty, commitment, partner

Dog + book (26): friend you need to get to know better, detective

Dog + letter (27): e-mails, text messaging, notes

Dog + man (28): soul mate, a man you know, a friend, a boyfriend, companion

Dog + woman (29): soul mate, a woman you know, girlfriend, companion

Dog + lily (30): old buddies, long-term friendships, father

Dog + sun (31): protective friend, father figure, benefactor

Dog + moon (32): motherly friend, romantic friendship, creative partner

Dog + key (33): soul mates, past life connection, savior

Dog + fish (34): colleagues, business partners, share holders

Dog + anchor (35): lifelong friendship, stable partnership

Dog + cross (36): confident, priest, support group

Footnotes:

This card will sometimes send a cryptic message. It may predict you will meet someone you already know even if you have no idea what it means and who it is. Later on you meet a prospect, but this individual is a complete stranger to you. Only to find out that you were both attending the same school 20 years earlier! So keep an open mind to the meanings of the dog.

The fourth group of cards is:

19. The tower: an old commanding tower guarding the entrance of the city

20. The garden: well-maintained garden welcoming strangers to relax

21. The mountain: a challenging mountain facing your destiny

22. The crossroad: two paths ahead splitting in different directions

23. The mice: rodents feeding over leftovers in dark alleys

24. The heart: a symbolic heart for lovers to share

19- The Tower

Keywords/meanings:
The tower guards and protects. It is typically a governmental institution such as the White House, the Pentagon or any other state, county, or military site. In the private sector, the card shows power and hierarchy of the corporate pyramid system. Commercial buildings associate themselves with the tower, particularly high rises and malls. Symbolically the card represents legal matters like judgments, liens and administrations such as the I.R.S, tax office or the Immigration Service. The tower is also an educative symbol often referring to colleges and universities, superior education and research. Everything that is official and important such as prisons, hospitals, airports, courthouses, banks are also an aspect of the tower. The building represents the ego, someone's ambitions and belief system.

Descriptions:
The tower person is tall (6 feet or taller), well-educated, who may feel superior morally and socially. This arrogance is part of the negative aspect of the card. Also, a person under this symbol has high expectations and ideals. Sometimes discriminating and egocentric, the tower personality can be overbearing. Certain types of professionals like judges, lawyers, executives, graduates and high rollers fall under the spectrum of the tower.

Astrological reference:
The ruler of the tower is Saturn (austerity).
The astrological sign is Capricorn - earth element - (December 21st to January 21st).

Associated Lenormand playing card:
Six of Spades

Special features:
In real estate questions, the tower encompasses office buildings, commercial outlets, movie theaters, condos and investment properties. Think height and large square footage.

Body connection:
The tower connects to the spine and the back.

Card associations:
Tower + horseman (1): acquisition, merger, new branch office
Tower + clover (2): promotional opportunity, prosperous corporation
Tower + ship (3): immigration agency, control tower, airport
Tower + house (4): housing agency, real estate, high rise apartment
Tower + tree (5): hospital, convalescent home, temple, spiritual center
Tower + clouds (6): error of judgment, troubled corporation, multi-national firm
Tower + snake (7): prison, legal problems, corporate corruption
Tower + coffin (8): cemetery, mortuary, corporate bankruptcy
Tower + bouquet (9): estate, architectural building, mall, national landmark
Tower + scythe (10): courthouse, destruction, ruins, judgment
Tower + whip (11): correctional facilities, fitness center, stadium
Tower + birds (12): amphitheater, congress, senate, assembly
Tower + child (13): child services, adoption agency, college
Tower + fox (14): corporation, executive position, corporate employee
Tower + bear (15): financial/banking institution, insurance company
Tower + star (16): movie studio, television studio, production company
Tower + storks (17): corporate growth, promotion to the top
Tower + dog (18): membership organization, corporate president, director

Tower + garden (20): network/professional organization, union, lobbyists

Tower + mountain (21): governmental agency, government bureaucracy

Tower + crossroad (22): corporate holdings, multiple agency company, franchise

Tower + mice (23): corporate losses, governmental fleecing

Tower + heart (24): charitable organization, humanitarian group

Tower + ring (25): stock market, national agency, United Nations

Tower + book (26): Internal Revenue Agency, taxes, FBI, CIA

Tower + letter (27): laws, constitution, regulations, legal notifications

Tower + man (28): tall, high roller, established individual, ambitious

Tower + woman (29): tall woman, top executive female, high morals, demanding

Tower + lily (30): senior management, trusts, conservancy, landmark

Tower + sun (31): monopoly, leadership position, king, president

Tower + moon (32): entertainment industry, design, architecture, special effects

Tower + key (33): world leadership, worldwide influence, divine power

Tower + fish (34): commerce, international trade, consulate, embassy

Tower + anchor (35): multi-generational company, estate trust, world landmark

Tower + cross (36): religious institutions, sites of worships, religions

Footnotes:
With the tower card, think big: big egos, big buildings, big goals, big power, etc.

20- The Garden

Keywords/meanings:
The garden translates into the general public, groups and crowds. This means parties, meetings, live events (concerts, carnivals), and social activities. The card may talk about non-profit organizations, charities and network marketing. But it is always associated with enjoyable circumstances. Think large numbers of people, numerous acquaintances, and audiences.

Descriptions:
A "garden" person is very active, social and popular. Sometimes a party animal, the individual is usually an altruist with pleasant qualities. You will notice the card representing advertising and public relation professionals very often. The symbol gives the ability to be a group leader, a philanthropist. Nature is a dominant attribute of the card so a lot of people under this influence are fond of gardening, visiting parks, walking, hiking and fishing.

Astrological reference:
The ruler of the garden is Venus (harmony).
The astrological signs are: Libra - air element - (September 21st to October 21st) and Sagittarius - fire element - (November 21st to December 21st).

Associated Lenormand playing card:
Eight of Spades

Special features:
The card hints on the possibility of classes, professional trainings, seminars. It also represents your entire network of people.

Body connection:
The garden refers to the immune system.

Card associations:

Garden + horseman (1): new acquaintances, new comers

Garden + clover (2): opportunities through networking, productive group

Garden + ship (3): foreigners, travelers, exotic plants

Garden + house (4): house party, guests, home with garden

Garden + tree (5): healthy, spiritual group, holistic lifestyle

Garden + clouds (6): crowd, demonstrations, audience, attendees

Garden + snake (7): trouble makers, disturbances, gang

Garden + coffin (8): rejection, expulsion, destruction

Garden + bouquet (9): happiness, contentment, bliss

Garden + scythe (10): group decisions, voting, jurors, market surveys

Garden + whip (11): team sports, harvest, agriculture, fields

Garden + birds (12): social gatherings, concerts, public events

Garden + child (13): playground, day care, scholars, students

Garden + fox (14): colleagues, work environment, work force

Garden + bear (15): catering, restaurants, food network

Garden + star (16): motivational workshops, group supports

Garden + storks (17): prosperity, growth, expansion

Garden + dog (18): celebration, reunion, gatherings

Garden + tower (19): high society, high rollers, royals

Garden + mountain (21): resistance, opposition, restrictions, limits

Garden + crossroad (22): multiple opportunities, extraordinary growth period

Garden + mice (23): discomfort, stressful network, excitements

Garden + heart (24): communion, marriage, engagement party

Garden + ring (25): marriage ceremony, meetings

Garden + book (26): group study, classes, students, library

Garden + letter (27): chat room, conference call, newsletter

Garden + man (28): popular individual, student, group member, network guy

Garden + woman (29): outdoor lover, social person, attendee, popular lady

Garden + lily (30): tranquility, Zen garden, spa, meditation space

Garden + sun (31): popular success, fame, fans, groupies

Garden + moon (32): premiere, celebrity party, creative event

Garden + key (33): important meeting, soul mates, karmic connections

Garden + fish (34): trade show, demonstration, industry union

Garden + anchor (35): serenity, satisfaction, stable prosperity

Garden+ cross (36): prayers, group support, therapy, recovery programs

Footnotes:

The garden is an indicator of someone's social abilities. It is most of the time a positive symbol, but with excess can portray an individual with a promiscuous behavior, and a lousy life style.

21- The Mountain

Keywords/meanings:
The mountain announces delays, stalled situations, obstacles that will slow down any enterprise. The card has a cold and distant effect on relationships creating walls in communication leading to rejection or indifference. It is quiet, silent and the only thing left is either waiting patiently or finding another way around the mountain. The symbol can predict a refusal or a state of denial. Sometimes it warns of an enemy, a danger, an insurmountable situation. This is the predator card.

Descriptions:
The individual under the influence of this card is cold, harsh, immovable or uncooperative. This distant person can be threatening by their presence or by their position in your life. The mountain can describe a humid, cold and dark climate like snowy pastures, stiff mountains and frozen lakes. All cool colors such as icy tones, blues, white, grays and silvers are associated with this card.

Astrological reference:
The ruler of the mountain is Saturn (isolation).
The astrological sign is Capricorn - earth element - (December 21st to January 21st).

Associated Lenormand playing card:
Eight of Clubs

Special features:
The mountain always delays any previously predicted time frames in readings. It also informs you of problems that may slow you down (3 weeks to a couple of months generally). And, in rare cases, the delay could be several months to several years!

Body connection:
The mountain represents the head.

Card associations:
Mountain + horseman (1): long awaited news, no more delay
Mountain + clover (2): new start, new momentum, things are picking up
Mountain + ship (3): exile, delayed travel, late plane
Mountain + house (4): isolation, loneliness, solitude, single parent
Mountain + tree (5): blockages creating health issues, immobilized, fatigued
Mountain + clouds (6): uncertainty, lost, unclear, procrastination
Mountain + snake (7): roadblocks, adversity, limitations
Mountain + coffin (8): end of delays, agony, dying, expiring
Mountain + bouquet (9): rest, vacation, park, mountains
Mountain + scythe (10): auto destructive habits or actions, pending decision
Mountain + whip (11): punishment, resistance training, mountain climbing
Mountain + birds (12): reconciliation, reunion, reconnection
Mountain + child (13): mentally challenged, slow development, isolated child
Mountain + fox (14): unemployment, leave of absence, sabbatical
Mountain + bear (15): famine, diet, bear, wild life
Mountain + star (16): procrastination, laziness, passive, unmotivated
Mountain + storks (17): moving on, re-energized, restart
Mountain + dog (18): longing, lonely, abandoned
Mountain + tower (19): imprisonment, locked, legal restrictions
Mountain + garden (20): vacation, retreat, mountain resort, spa
Mountain + crossroad (22): excursion, expedition, hiking, skiing
Mountain + mice (23): frustrations, exasperation, failures
Mountain + heart (24): artery restriction, emotionally indifferent, lonely
Mountain + ring (25): restrained, responsibilities, obligations

Mountain + book (26): study, internship, apprentice, monastery

Mountain + letter (27): unreachable, unresponsive, slow response

Mountain + man (28): enemy, distant individual, indifferent, uncommunicative

Mountain + woman (29): lonely woman, unresponsive, resistant, unwilling

Mountain + lily (30): retirement, retreat, remote location, snow

Mountain + sun (31): long awaited success, volcano, desert canyon

Mountain + moon (32): emotionally disconnected, insensitive, fear of intimacy

Mountain + key (33): significant waiting period, delay designed by fate

Mountain + fish (34): island, fish and game, nature oriented business

Mountain + anchor (35): permanent, long-term, immovable, forever

Mountain + cross (36): victimized, weakness, phobias, depression

Footnotes:

The mountain should always be translated as a delay of some sort. Extend your estimated time frame accordingly in order to be more accurate in your predictions.

22- The Crossroad

Keywords/meanings:

The picture brings choices and decisions in one's life. The two paths ahead offer either an escape or the option to run away from a situation, or a junction as a solution to a problem. The presented options nevertheless need serious evaluation which may lead to a life crisis. The crossroad means multiples as well (girlfriends, lives, jobs etc). It also brings mediation (divorce, lawsuit and other) to issues, new alternatives to stalled situations. The crossroad is about several opportunities and the exercise of the ultimate human power: free will.

Descriptions:

The crossroad portrays individuals very successful with 'double talk' and often with potentially unstable personalities. The frame of mind can be constantly hesitant, uncertain about life or in the middle of a life crisis. On a positive note, someone described with this picture may be very well-versed in diplomacy. People with careers in mediation will appear through the symbol. Multi-task professionals who are trouble shooters will also be a part of the crossroad concept. When you see this picture, you should think diversification, multiple, and plural, to help you understand the meaning. Reminder: it is the escape card so be aware of fugitives from the law! Physically crossroad people are likely to have reddish highlights or red colored hair with medium to fair skin.

Astrological reference:

The ruler of the crossroad is Uranus (opportunity).
The astrological sign is Libra - air element - (September 21st to October 21st).

Associated Lenormand playing card:

Queen of Diamonds

Special features:
This card can estimate a time frame of 2 weeks, 2 months or 2 years when it appears.

Body connection:
The crossroad describes the arteries.

Card associations:
Crossroad + horseman (1): counter offer, news helping in decision making

Crossroad + clover (2): lucky break, escape, good fortune in new endeavors

Crossroad + ship (3): multiple travels ahead, road trip

Crossroad + house (4): multiple residences, real estate investments, duplex

Crossroad + tree (5): karmic connections, past life regression, spiritual journey

Crossroad + clouds (6): extreme confusion, clouded judgment, futility

Crossroad + snake (7): road problems, tough choices, complications

Crossroad + coffin (8): dead end, options leading no where, negative outcome

Crossroad + bouquet (9): multiple hobbies and interests, large network

Crossroad + scythe (10): accidents, turning down an offer, decision

Crossroad + whip (11): promiscuous, marathon runner, bicycle trip

Crossroad + birds (12): multiple meetings or interviews, board of directors

Crossroad + child (13): twins, siblings, multiple births, in vitro fertility treatment

Crossroad + fox (14): part time or multiple jobs, truck driver, road construction job

Crossroad + bear (15): multiple incomes, diversified financial portfolio

Crossroad + star (16): leader, guide, general, commander

Crossroad + stork (17): improvements, progress, advancements

Crossroad + dog (18): friends, running partners, split in friendship

Crossroad + tower (19): legal mediation, bridge, metropolis, freeways

Crossroad + garden (20): excursion, tour, multiple public events

Crossroad + mountain (21): delayed outcomes, unable to make a choice

Crossroad + mice (23): exciting opportunities, exhaustion, fatigue, incoherence

Crossroad + heart (24): dating, uncommitted, playboy, promiscuous

Crossroad + ring (25): commitment, settling down, agreement, reunion

Crossroad + book (26): clues, exploration, chapters, trusts

Crossroad + letter (27): mailing, marketing list, dispatching information

Crossroad + man (28): negotiator, open minded individual, hesitant, in transition

Crossroad + woman (29): unsettled woman, double talker, unsure

Crossroad + lily (30): walking around, choice bringing serenity, peace at last

Crossroad + sun (31): successful choices, good fortune, great outcome

Crossroad + moon (32): emotional indecision, creative outlets, passions

Crossroad + key (33): life turning point, destiny, significant decision

Crossroad + fish (34): adventures, trade route, multiple businesses

Crossroad + anchor (35): independence, confidence, unstable lifestyle

Crossroad + cross (36): pilgrimage, spiritual crisis, painful choices

Footnotes:

With this card, the issue between free will and fate is revealed. In the reading one has a choice, but the outcome may be difficult to predict accurately. What one should do and what one actually does do are not always the same. The human factor is the wild card, as our choices of today determine our future tomorrows.

23- The Mice

Keywords/meanings:

The mice announce stressful times with the following side effects: nervousness, exhaustion, anxiety, worries. They bring losses of any kind as well as cause sadness, grief, frustration and sometimes a pattern of destruction. The picture also shows busy pests symbolizing labor and therefore the manufacturing process, the spirit of teamwork and labor workers. The industrial sector fits this card well. Closer to home, the mice uncover hidden problems such as leaks, mold, spoiled food and diseases. With regard to the mind, it may intimate feelings of being lost, fatigued, sick or annoyed. Mental weakness such as loss of memory is also a possible side effect. Overall the mice are never a good omen.

Descriptions:

The behavior under this card could be referred to as passive aggressive, destructive, and laborious. Most likely in a reading it will indicate an overworked, anxious person with a lot of problems to cope with. People with Attention Deficit Disorder (ADD) may surface through this symbol as well.

Astrological reference:

The rulers of the mice are Saturn (austerity) and Uranus (changes).

Associated Lenormand playing card:

Seven of Clubs

Special features:

The mice can indicate a time frame referring to hours or days, rarely weeks.

Body connection:

The mice are the nervous system.

Card associations:

Mice + horseman (1): apprehension toward new situations, anticipation

Mice + clover (2): excitements, butterflies, nervousness

Mice + ship (3): mechanical problems, used vehicle

Mice + house (4): structural problems, fixing required in the house (i.e. plumbing)

Mice + tree (5): stress related illness, depressing thoughts, fatigue

Mice + clouds (6): lost, nervous breakdown, confusion, destructive behavior

Mice + snake (7): overwhelmed, extreme difficulties, unable to cope

Mice + coffin (8): no more stress, calming down, relief

Mice + bouquet (9): fervor, enthusiasm, excitements

Mice + scythe (10): stressful decisions, seizures, rushed judgment

Mice + whip (11): chronicle anxiety, physical stress, convulsions, cramps

Mice + birds (12): verbal confusion, therapy, speech disorder, wrangling

Mice + child (13): hyperactive child, attention deficit problem, restless kid

Mice + fox (14): stressful job, uncertain employment, degrading work

Mice + bear (15): financial loss, cash flow struggle, out of control spending

Mice + star (16): exciting opportunity, stressful goals, under pressure

Mice + stork (17): stressful move, unwanted changes, laborious progress

Mice + dog (18): draining relationships, stressful friends, oppressing partner

Mice + tower (19): legal troubles, government mismanagement

Mice + garden (20): relaxing entertainment, spa, relief, public demonstration

Mice + mountain (21): giving up, despair, resignation, stressful delay

Mice + crossroad (22): division, mental confusion, denial, oblivious

Mice + heart (24): palpitations, heartaches, infatuation, emotional stress

Mice + ring (25): difficult resolution, fixing a situation, unreliable commitment

Mice + book (26): secrets, fear of the unknown, depreciation

Mice + letter (27): stressful news, poor communication

Mice + man (28): destructive individual, stressed, nervous, unstable man

Mice + woman (29): tense lady, anxious, overworked, weak

Mice + lily (30): aging problems, tremors, shaking

Mice + sun (31): hard to reach success, challenging victory

Mice + moon (32): mood swings, emotional distress, nervousness

Mice + key (33): recovery, replacement

Mice + fish (34): business challenges, loss of customers, slow activity

Mice + anchor (35): challenging situation, stressful lifestyle, courage

Mice + cross (36): suffering, grief, serious anxiety, fears

Footnotes:

The mice can be a serious health warning depending on your inquiry. Over a long period of time, stress can lead to much more significant illnesses. Learning to manage difficult times can be a life savior. Do not sweat the small stuff!

24- The Heart

Keywords/meanings:
The heart predicts a time for love and romance, tenderness, generosity and passion. It creates loving and sensual relationships, puppy loves and platonic romances. The symbol is the act of giving, caring for others (donations, humanitarian work, and philanthropy) and about feelings.

Descriptions:
The card may portray a compassionate person who is emotionally demonstrative and sensual. Usually heart people physically display light brown or blonde hair. All red, pink, and orange colors are represented through this card.

Astrological reference:
The ruler of the heart is Venus (love).

Associated Lenormand playing card:
Jack of Hearts

Special features:
This card may forecast a future lover, the next romantic relationship or the love of a life time. But, it is not an indicator of marriage and commitment. The ring is!

Body connection:
The picture is of the heart and the blood vessels.

Card associations:
Heart + horseman (1): new relationship opportunity, new lover
Heart + clover (2): prosperous relationship, lucky in love
Heart + ship (3): romantic trip, honeymoon, foreign lover
Heart + house (4): couple living together, family life, loving family
Heart + tree (5): soul mate connection, spiritual love, karmic romance
Heart + clouds (6): deceptive relationship, troubled lover, untruthful
Heart + snake (7): cheating, relationship problems, betrayal, deceit
Heart + coffin (8): end of a love, end of relationship, loss of a lover
Heart + bouquet (9): happy relationship, promising love, handsome lover
Heart + scythe (10): emotional break up, decision affecting a relationship
Heart + whip (11): sexual co-dependency, passionate love, sexual passion
Heart + birds (12): romance, couple, lovers, life partner
Heart + child (13): immature lover, college sweetheart, love child
Heart + fox (14): deceptive relationship, professional passion, emotional work
Heart + bear (15): generous relationship, wealthy lover, protective partner
Heart + star (16): positive relationship, falling in love, inspiring love
Heart + stork (17): growing relationship, family planning
Heart + dog (18): friends and lovers, special friend, best friends
Heart + tower (19): ambitious relationship, tall lover, power couple
Heart + garden (20): outgoing relationship, multiple partners, open relations
Heart + mountain (21): stalling romance, indifference, falling out of love

Heart + crossroad (22): separation, multiple lovers, time out, uncommitted

Heart + mice (23): dying relationship, stressful romance, overwhelming love

Heart + ring (25): marriage, commitment, life partner, union

Heart + book (26): secret affair, unfulfilled romance, hidden crush

Heart + letter (27): love letters, news from a lover

Heart + man (28): lover, caring man, compassionate individual, generous

Heart + woman (29): lover, loving woman, gentle, passionate

Heart + lily (30): mature lover, later in life romance, long-term relationship

Heart + sun (31): happy and successful romance, charismatic relationship

Heart + moon (32): happy romantic relationship, intimacy

Heart + key (33): significant relationship, influential lover, soul mate

Heart + fish (34): dating game, single scene, matchmaker

Heart + anchor (35): steady relationship, long-term romance

Heart + cross (36): relationship insecurities, heartaches, emotional pains

Footnotes:

The heart is central to find out what motivate two people to be together. Negative cards around it may warn against a lack of real feelings in a romance. The card reveals the future of your love life as well as the present status of your relationship.

The fifth group of cards is:

25. The ring: a solitaire ring displayed on a dark velvet cloth

26. The book: a mysterious leather covered book open to reveal secrets

27. The letter: a sealed envelop hiding important words

28. The man: a noble gentleman standing by

29. The woman: an attractive lady in waiting

30. The lily: a beautiful set of lilies gracefully displayed

25- The Ring

Keywords/meanings:

The ring embraces all contracts, agreements and deals of all sorts. Of course among those, marriage and civil union are important ones. Typically the card talks about being together in a committed relationship. The notorious engagement ring symbolizes the offer, the proposal, the involvement between two people, but also the agreement, the contract between two parties. This card is a gift, a present, a reunion, an approval between individuals. The aspect of completion represented by the circle gives a positive answer, a satisfying solution (full circle) to any concern.

Descriptions:

As a personality trait, a "ring" individual brings predictability, stability and seriousness in the intentions. Most are straight shooters who are generally accountable for their actions. This quality makes them dependable and loyal.

Astrological reference:

The ruler of the ring is Venus (harmony).
The astrological sign is Taurus - earth element - (April 21st to May 21st).

Associated Lenormand playing card:

Ace of Clubs

Special features:

If you ask about the marital status of a person and the ring appears, the thought should be that the object of your inquiry may be unavailable at this point of time. When the picture appears spontaneously next to the person card it confirms that this individual is attached to a situation or a relationship i.e. married, engaged, involved or committed to another. A background check should ultimately help confirm the insight if necessary.

Body connection:
The ring is the lymphatic system.

Card associations:
Ring + horseman (1): new partner, new member
Ring + clover (2): safe opportunity, stable growth
Ring + ship (3): international business contract, permanent resident visa
Ring + house (4): real estate transaction (sale, purchase or lease)
Ring + tree (5): expansion, branching out, growth, healing
Ring + clouds (6): convoluted transaction, suspicious agreement
Ring + snake (7): difficult transaction, disagreement
Ring + coffin (8): voided contract, marriage dissolution, rescind
Ring + bouquet (9): pleasant transaction, positive outcome
Ring + scythe (10): breach of contract, divorce
Ring + whip (11): disputes, disagreements, divorce
Ring + birds (12): negotiations, mediations, sale meetings
Ring + child (13): adoption, legitimate offspring, fertile union
Ring + fox (14): employment contract, work schedule
Ring + bear (15): financial transactions, sales, profits, contracts
Ring + star (16): promising agreement, investments
Ring + stork (17): raise, promotion, increase, expansion
Ring + dog (18): partner, spouse, associate, member
Ring + tower (19): legal judgment, courthouse, trial, prison
Ring + garden (20): large reunion, assembly, workshop
Ring + mountain (21): stalling agreement, hard to reach solution, impasse
Ring + crossroad (22): split, separation, breaking up, division
Ring + mice (23): contract leading to losses, dismantling
Ring + heart (24): marriage, committed love, civil union
Ring + book (26): investigation, report, analysis, audit
Ring + letter (27): promissory note, contract, written agreement
Ring + man (28): husband, partner, fiancé, a man of his words
Ring + woman (29): wife, partner, fiancée, loyal companion
Ring + lily (30): long-term contract or lifetime partnership, old agreement

Ring + sun (31): prestigious contract, successful partnership, victory

Ring + moon (32): emotional bond, famous partnership, award

Ring + key (33): karmic partnership, past life bond, soul mate

Ring + fish (34): business transaction, trade agreement, business partnership

Ring + anchor (35): stable association, long-term agreement

Ring + cross (36): bondage, unpleasant association, regrettable dealing

Footnotes:

The ring can tell about a relationship's future. It is an important card for any romantic inquiry to know if the prospect you have met could be a reliable partner. It also unveils any unavailable individual regardless of what the appearance may show. You should trust the ring to reveal the true emotional life of a person.

26- The Book

Keywords/meanings:

The book represents the unknown, the occult. It symbolizes projects, cases, discoveries and studies: it may be confidential information subject to an indiscretion, a project to create, a case study to analyze or an assignment to undertake. The picture talks about general education or specialized training such as esoteric studies. The book brings experience and professional expertise because it infers in-depth knowledge. Reading, learning, writing and analyzing are activities contained in the message. Finally, the symbol could forecast a surprise, an unforeseen event to shake life's routine and promote personal knowledge.

Descriptions:

Educated, intelligent and resourceful people are shown through this picture. The professional described can be a screenwriter, a scholar, an editor, a graduate, an investigator or private eye, a chemist or a teacher. The individual will most likely have a career that requires a degree or professional license. The "book" person is discreet, curious, and knowledgeable with excellent memory skills.

Astrological reference:

The rulers of the book are Saturn (teacher) and Mercury (communication).
The astrological sign is Virgo - earth element - (August 21st to September 21st).

Associated Lenormand playing card:

Ten of Diamonds

Special features:

The book may sometimes appear to warn that something completely unexpected will occur. The event will be significant as it will teach some life lessons or promote personal growth.

Body connection:
The book connects to the brain.

Card associations:
Book + horseman (1): revelations, additional facts, new
  unexpected situations
Book + clover (2): surprising discovery, lucky find, break through
Book + ship (3): expedition, foreign language, study abroad,
  cultural trip
Book + house (4): real estate knowledge, real estate agent,
  architect
Book + tree (5): spiritual/holistic studies, medical training,
  herbalist
Book + clouds (6): mental confusion, misleading information,
  mental disorder
Book + snake (7): lies, deceptive practice, learning disorders,
  disinformation
Book + coffin (8): drop out, illiterate, uneducated, ignorance
Book + bouquet (9): cosmetic/beauty expert, women studies,
  hair stylist
Book + scythe (10): interrupted studies, surgical internship,
  medical examiner
Book + whip (11): physical therapy studies, sex education
Book + birds (12): communication training, media expertise
Book + child (13): student, children studies, social studies, child
  psychologist
Book + fox (14): teacher, professor, consultant, detective,
  librarian
Book + bear (15): accounting studies, investment expert,
  nutrition consultant/chef
Book + star (16): visual arts studies, computer training,
  technology expert
Book + stork (17): graduation, coaching, training, final exams
Book + dog (18): class mate, advisor, paralegal, consultant
Book + tower (19): legal studies, law degree, college, university
Book + garden (20): poetry, novel, workshops, classes

Book + mountain (21): intellectually challenged, nature studies, geologist

Book + crossroad (22): multiple degrees or certifications, extensive studies

Book + mice (23): poor memory, micro-biologist, lab student, tedious studies

Book + heart (24): secret crush, secret lover, affair, cardiologist

Book + ring (25): graduate, honor student, diploma, jeweler

Book + letter (27): application, diploma, certification, license

Book + man (28): educated man, analytical, intelligent, secretive

Book + woman (29): smart woman, discreet, knowledgeable, researcher

Book + lily (30): history or archeology studies, expertise, post graduate

Book + sun (31): physics, mathematical studies, brilliant mind

Book + moon (32): psychology studies, esoteric knowledge, psychic

Book + key (33): Nobel Prize, world recognition, invention, discovery

Book + fish (34): marketing studies, business degree, marine life expert

Book + anchor (35): professional student, marine corp., naval expert

Book + cross (36): religious studies, spiritual training, grief counselor

Footnotes:

People who appear with the book are sometimes hiding very important information about themselves and their lives. It is up to you to discover their secrets. Knowledge is power!

27- The Letter

Keywords/meanings:
The picture brings news through the form of letters, e-mails, faxes or any kind of paper format information. The message is on its way and coming soon. The press or any written paper media have a "letter" quality. The card can sometimes represent an invoice, a certified mail, a sealed document, a will or a power of attorney. The documents may be confidential or ready to be public. Also the letter refers to tangible signs of appreciation such as awards, trophies and diplomas.

Descriptions:
The "letter" individuals are usually very communicative with specific information. College graduates, award winners, certified or licensed professionals appear with this picture, and they usually display their achievements with great pride.

Astrological reference:
The ruler of the letter is Mercury (communication).

Associated Lenormand playing card:
Seven of Spades

Special features:
The letter is about paper trail, physical forms of communication in contrast to the birds who deal with verbal communication.

Body connection:
The letter symbolizes the hands and fingers.

Card associations:

Letter + horseman (1): additional information, response, feedback

Letter + clover (2): lottery, sweepstakes

Letter + ship (3): international mail, news from far away, package

Letter + house (4): property title, real estate contract, home owner insurance

Letter + tree (5): life or health insurance policy, will, spiritual message

Letter + clouds (6): confusing messages, scattered news

Letter + snake (7): troublesome letter, bad news, complaint

Letter + coffin (8): condolences, shredding of documents

Letter + bouquet (9): happy announcements, party invitation, post card

Letter + scythe (10): interruption in correspondence, letter returned to sender

Letter + whip (11): angry letters, erotic correspondence, forwarded letter

Letter + birds (12): active pen pals, newsletter, writers group, bloggers

Letter + child (13): birth announcement, baby shower invitation

Letter + fox (14): employment contract, pay check

Letter + bear (15): check, cash, bonds, invoices

Letter + star (16): hopeful news, astronomy degree, astrological charts

Letter + stork (17): updates, follow ups, support letters

Letter + dog (18): pen pal, internet friend, instant messaging

Letter + tower (19): legal notice, default notice, mortgage, tax return

Letter + garden (20): marketing mail, client list, newsletter

Letter + mountain (21): delayed letter, snail mail, message not received yet

Letter + crossroad (22): mass mailing, marketing campaign

Letter + mice (23): stressful news, junk mail, lost letter

Letter + heart (24): internet romance, love letters

Letter + ring (25): contract, written agreement, payment

Letter + book (26): audit, accounting records, reports

Letter + man (28): writer, licensed professional, certified

Letter + woman (29): graduate, award winner, published individual

Letter + lily (30): news from parents, outdated information, photos

Letter + sun (31): enthusiastic letter, award, trophy

Letter + moon (32): romantic letters, poems, creative prints

Letter + key (33): important letter, vital records

Letter + fish (34): business documents, customs, orders

Letter + anchor (35): encouraging news, will, living trust

Letter + cross (36): grievance, painful news, troubling information

Footnotes:

This card gives proof of our correspondence. It is the physical representation of our communication with others. Thus, the letter is any kind of documentation such as fax, e-mail, text message.

28- The Man

Keywords/meanings:
This card personifies a man who could be the person you are interested in, a stranger about to enter your life or just a representation of yourself if you are a male. The man symbol is always neutral. In order to understand the card's significance, you will need to look into the meanings of the cards surrounding it.

Descriptions:
This unidentified individual may be a father, a husband, a lover, a son, a brother or a male acquaintance. To get a physical description you should look at the next card or the previous one. Some cards give hair colors, eye colors, height and build. Some give moral and intellectual traits that could be interesting. Finally specific cards next to this male representation could reveal his marital status and his emotional availability.

Astrological reference:
The ruler of the man is the Sun (masculine symbol).

Associated Lenormand playing card:
Ace of Heart

Special features:
You can mentally attach a first name onto this representation to symbolize the person you want to know about (male). The card will then take on the vibrations of the individual and will provide information you need to know. In order to have an accurate reading, your concentration and focus during the process is essential. By assigning a name onto the man card you are "charging" it with the essence of the person in question. The surrounding cards will then give you the answers.

Card associations:

Man + horseman (1): Fit and outgoing male bringing novelty into your life

Man + clover (2): new beneficial individual who likes to take risks, opportunist

Man + ship (3): well-traveled, foreigner, with dark hair or/and dark eyes

Man + house (4): family man, landlord, real estate owner, stable

Man + tree (5): religious or spiritual, health conscious individual

Man + clouds (6): multiple personality individual, unstable, confused

Man + snake (7): trouble maker, man in crisis, liar, deceitful

Man + coffin (8): negative thinker, depressed

Man + bouquet (9): good looking guy, smiling and charming, nice disposition

Man + scythe (10): decision maker, abrasive personality, swift

Man + whip (11): abusive, aggressive behavior, very fit, sexual

Man + birds (12): companion, easy communicator, social, eloquent

Man + child (13): immature, adolescent, young looking

Man + fox (14): workaholic, sneaky, dishonest

Man + bear (15): powerful, protective, controlling, facial hair

Man + star (16): famous person, dreamer, tech guy, inspiring

Man + stork (17): progressive individual, self-made, open minded

Man + dog (18): friend, partner, husband, a man you already know

Man + tower (19): strong moral values, ambitious, egocentric, tall

Man + garden (20): popular, social, party oriented, fun

Man + mountain (21): single man, loner, asocial, shy

Man + crossroad (22): double-life, unstable, commitment phobic

Man + mice (23): low self esteem, anxious, stressed, self-destructive

Man + heart (24): generous, emotionally open, boyfriend

Man + ring (25): married, involved/engaged, unavailable, husband

Man + book (26): educated, graduate, intelligent, secretive

Man + letter (27): message from a man, postman, published individual, reporter

Man + woman (29): a couple, relationship, connection, meeting

Man + lily (30): elderly male, experienced, established individual, mature

Man + sun (31): successful, egoist, competitive, survivor

Man + moon (32): artistic, creative, sensitive, psychic

Man + key (33): soul mate, remarkable individual, important person in your life

Man + fish (34): business man, wheeler dealer, entrepreneurial, salesman

Man + anchor (35): stable, dependable, loyal

Man + cross (36): distressed, victim mentality, needy

Footnotes:

The man is a symbol that needs other cards to have meanings and information. Check the surrounding cards to profile the stranger and understand his purpose in your life.

29- The Woman

Keywords/meanings:
This card represents a woman who could be the person you are asking about, a stranger coming into your life or just a symbol of yourself, if you are a female. The woman picture is neutral and will take more meanings depending on the cards surrounding it.

Descriptions:
The picture may be symbolizing a mother, a wife, a mistress, a daughter, a relative or a female friend. You should pay attention to the cards before and next to it to profile the unidentified individual. Depending on the meanings of each card you may have a physical or character description.

Astrological reference:
The ruler of the woman is the Moon (feminine).

Associated Lenormand playing card:
Ace of Spades

Special features:
The woman card is needed to capture the essence -vibrations- of the female you have questions about. The symbol is "charged" with the psychic energies of the lady by focusing on the picture and by assigning the card her first name (or full name). This crucial process allows the card to become "alive" in the reading. The surrounding cards will then provide accurate information regarding her life or details on her physical appearance and/or character.

Card associations:

Woman + horseman (1): new relationship with an attractive man

Woman + clover (2): positive attitude, opportunist, gold-digger

Woman + ship (3): woman born or educated abroad, flight attendant, exotic look

Woman + house (4): housewife, landlady, family oriented, stable

Woman + tree (5): religious or spiritual, soul mate connection, healthy

Woman + clouds (6): emotionally unstable, scattered, confused

Woman + snake (7): troubled female, difficult, high maintenance

Woman + coffin (8): depressed or negative thinker, draining personality

Woman + bouquet (9): attractive, pleasant, balanced individual, happy

Woman + scythe (10): decision maker, dry personality, leader

Woman + whip (11): passive aggressive, fit and active, sexual

Woman + birds (12): companion, wife, friend, good communicator

Woman + child (13): single mother, girl, immature, capricious, petite

Woman + fox (14): workaholic, employed, sneaky, deceptive

Woman + bear (15): motherly, curvy, protective, strong, controlling

Woman + star (16): famous, role model, inspiring, scientist

Woman + stork (17): self-made, open minded

Woman + dog (18): confident, friend/companion, reliable, familiar

Woman + tower (19): ambitious, self centered, high achiever, tall

Woman + garden (20): social, happy, popular, party girl

Woman + mountain (21): single woman, loner, distant, reserved

Woman + crossroad (22): commitment challenged, unstable, promiscuous

Woman + mice (23): stressed, low self-esteem, annoying personality

Woman + heart (24): generous, lover, wife, girlfriend, loving

Woman + ring (25): married, committed/engaged or unavailable, wife

Woman + book (26): secretive, educated, inquisitive, stranger

Woman + letter (27): message from a female, mail lady

Woman + man (28): a couple relationship, connection, meeting

Woman + lily (30): elderly woman, mature, experienced

Woman + sun (31): career driven, successful, charismatic

Woman + moon (32): charming, creative/artistic, sensitive, psychic

Woman + key (33): soul mate, significant female, important relationship

Woman + fish (34): entrepreneur, business woman, resourceful

Woman + anchor (35): stable, reliable, confident personality

Woman + cross (36): woman in crisis, distressed, lonely, hurt

Footnotes:

It is important to look into the surrounding cards to understand the message of the reading. The woman card can personify a complete stranger or someone you already know. The cards next to the woman card will tell you more about her.

30- The Lily

Keywords/meanings:
The lily brings peace and contentment. It is the satisfaction in having finished a task, completed a project or reached an emotional goal. The card is also the sign of maturity and wisdom. It is the professional experience or the life-long history that you may be offering to others. The lily is the Zen factor in a reading, a sense of completion bringing total serenity in one's life.

Descriptions:
The card announces a mature, older individual, generally successful and established in life. "Lily" people are calm, stable, wise and fatherly. The lily (generally masculine) may describe a father figure, an older brother, a grand father or a mature boyfriend. However, sometimes it symbolizes an older woman. All the dark gray and white colors are associated with it.

Astrological reference:
The ruler of the lily is Saturn (wisdom).
The astrological sign is Capricorn - earth element - (December 21st to January 21st).
The season is winter.

Associated Lenormand playing card:
King of Spades

Special features:
The lily announces a very slow pace in a reading because it is synonymous with the winter season. Therefore it predicts weeks or years in the development of a situation. The contemplation while waiting through the process has spiritual values that need to be understood.

Body connection:
The lily is the eyes/vision and the ears/hearing.

Card associations:
Lily + horseman (1): change of pace through new information, renewal, new cycle

Lily + clover (2): positive period, enjoyable retirement, senior benefits

Lily + ship (3): cruise, restful vacation, snowy destination, winter trip

Lily + house (4): landmark residence, old house, historical place, nursing home

Lily + tree (5): aging pains, meditation, yoga, serenity

Lily + clouds (6): discomfort, uncertain times, senile, lost

Lily + snake (7): resentment, bitterness, meanness, difficult elder

Lily + coffin (8): passing, fading away, ending

Lily + bouquet (9): contentment, joy, happiness

Lily + scythe (10): accident, fall, injury

Lily + whip (11): passive aggressive, stubborn pain, yoga, tai chi

Lily + birds (12): wisdom, mentor, elderly couple, counseling

Lily + child (13): oldest, only child, mature adolescent

Lily + fox (14): job experience, long-term employee, senior clerk

Lily + bear (15): bonds, retirement accounts, pensions, annuities

Lily + star (16): life achievement, famous senior, life recognition

Lily + stork (17): improvements, active elder, upgrade

Lily + dog (18): lifelong friendship, life companion, elderly friend

Lily + tower (19): convalescence home, retirement home, hospice

Lily + garden (20): senior community, senior gathering, spiritual class

Lily + mountain (21): immobilized, handicapped, coma

Lily + crossroad (22): hobbies, busy retirement

Lily + mice (23): memory lapse, mental diseases linked to aging

Lily + heart (24): mature romance, elderly couple, older companion

Lily + ring (25): late marriage, life long marriage, retirement benefits

Lily + book (26): extensive knowledge, librarian, encyclopedia, vintage

Lily + letter (27): photos, old documents, archives, vital records

Lily + man (28): older male, father, grand father, protector, mentor

Lily + woman (29): older female, mother, grandma, wise

Lily + sun (31): hall of fame, established success, late achievement

Lily + moon (32): psychic abilities, medium, clairvoyant, visionary

Lily + key (33): synchronicities, destiny, signs

Lily + fish (34): generation business, industries marketing to seniors

Lily + anchor (35): legacy, trust, heritance, life insurance

Lily + cross (36): depression, agony, longing, dependent

Footnotes:

The lily talks about our parents, our elders and the aging process. But, most likely, it will signal an older person or describe someone with gray hair.

The sixth group is:

31. The sun: sunrise bringing light and warmth to the Earth

32. The moon: guiding moon shining through the night

33. The key: an enigmatic key to decode

34. The fish: deep in the ocean fish follow currents and boats

35. The anchor: an anchor well set in the sandy shore

36. The cross: an ornate cross of gold and precious tones stands

31- The Sun

Keywords/meanings:
This picture brings success and happiness into any reading. It is the victory you have been waiting for. The sun symbolizes fame, glory, charisma, grandeur. It is a virile card centered on the ego. The energy generated by the sun associates with the tropics, the warmth of summer and the heat of the desert.

Descriptions:
Sun individuals display a lot of charisma and big smiling faces. Sun males are virile, protective and attractive. Famous personalities and established individuals usually come with it. But the darker side of the sun is also egocentricity, selfishness and overbearing energy. Sun people are usually fair colored (blonde, light brown, red) with very seductive attributes. All yellow and red colors are represented.

Astrological reference:
The sun (success) will be at home with the card bearing its name. All the fire signs could be connected with the sun:
Aries (March 21st to April 21st), Leo (July 21st to August 21st) and Sagittarius (November 21st to December 21st). The ruler of Leo being the sun the July/August period makes it a likely time reference in readings.

Associated Lenormand playing card:
Ace of Diamonds

Special features:
The sun indicates summer time therefore you can use that period as a time frame to predict an event. You can also use the fire signs for the same purpose of prediction.

Body connection:
The sun connects with the body energy and the solar plexus.

Card associations:

Sun + horseman (1): someone is coming to greet you, encounter

Sun + clover (2): incredible luck, good fortune, great synchronicities

Sun + ship (3): international success, summer vacation, hot destination

Sun + house (4): southern home, luxurious lifestyle, pride of ownership

Sun + tree (5): healthy, strong vitality, energetic, spiritual leader

Sun + clouds (6): success based on deception or lies, temporary success

Sun + snake (7): double-edged success, success bringing troubles

Sun + coffin (8): danger ahead, pit fall, reversal of fortune

Sun + bouquet (9): enjoyable success, pleasures, arts, collectibles

Sun + scythe (10): positive decisions, appropriate actions, victory

Sun + whip (11): exercise, sexual activity, competition, championship

Sun + birds (12): brilliant speaker, charismatic, actor, singer

Sun + child (13): boy, energetic kid, honor student, winner

Sun + fox (14): great career, corporate officer, top executive

Sun + bear (15): financial success, millionaire, venture capitalist, president

Sun + star (16): celebrity, leading personality, historical figure

Sun + stork (17): significant progress, fast success

Sun + dog (18): great buddy, well-known friend, father/mentor

Sun + tower (19): arena, amphitheater, stage, utility company, governments

Sun + garden (20): public, crowd, assembly, social event

Sun + mountain (21): forgotten personality, fading away, unattainable

Sun + crossroad (22): diversification, expansion, growth

Sun + mice (23): excitement, burned out, fatigue, diminished, tarnished

Sun + heart (24): passions, intense love relationship

Sun + ring (25): happy marriage, powerful partnership, successful contract

Sun + book (26): academic success, published research, patented invention

Sun + letter (27): medal, certification, acceptance letter

Sun + man (28): successful, achiever, winner

Sun + woman (29): vibrant woman, charismatic, strong, leader

Sun + lily (30): long lasting reputation, antiques, art collection

Sun + moon (32): "perfect couple", attraction, great compatibility

Sun + key (33): twist of fate, unexpected success, incredible luck

Sun + fish (34): successful business, positive venture, good fortune

Sun + anchor (35): legacy, long-term success, empire

Sun + cross (36): nervousness, apprehension, burns

Footnotes:
This is a powerful card influencing the reading in a very positive manner and giving one the energy necessary to brave any obstacle. The sun is the card of courage and overcoming adversity to reach your goals.

32- The Moon

Keywords/meanings:
The moon connects with our emotions and feelings (affection). It is the mother symbol that nurtures our souls and makes us feel loved. The picture opens the door to fantasies, dreams and romances. The games of seduction, the romantic attraction in a relationship appear under the moon. The moon is an evening muse to our senses (erotic), liberating our creativity and imagination. It also represents the arts, the entertainment and creative fields. The symbol pairs itself with fame, reputation and the world of celebrities. Finally, the moon reveals our spiritual life and the strength of our intuitive feelings and psychic abilities.

Descriptions:
The moon person is seductive and feminine, well-aware of her/his charms. Hypnotic and perceptive, the personality is soft and loving. Most artistic people will appear as moon because of the creativity they generate. The card will also relate to famous and well-recognized professionals. The physical description tends to refer to curvy bodies, fair or blond hair coloring. The attributes are caring, affectionate and motherly. All silver and metallic colors fall under the moon meanings.

Astrological reference:
The moon (emotions) rules itself.
The moon pairs with all the water signs which are:
Pisces (February 21st to March 21st), Cancer (June 21st to July 21st), Scorpio (October 21st to November 21st).
Because the moon rules Cancer, June and July will most likely be the time reference in a reading.

Associated Lenormand playing card:
Eight of Hearts

Special features:
The moon has a very fast time frame which can be hours, days or weeks. You can also use the water signs as time reference to predict when an event might take place.

Body connection:
The picture refers to the female organs and the hormonal system.

Card associations:
Moon + horseman (1): new romance, new boyfriend
Moon + clover (2): happy life, emotional thrill, positive outlook
Moon + ship (3): honeymoon, romantic getaway, foreign lover
Moon + house (4): customized home, dream home, temple
Moon + tree (5): feminine health, emotional life, mental health
Moon + clouds (6): romantic confusion, denial, emotional
   instability
Moon + snake (7): emotional deceit, romantic problems, upset
Moon + coffin (8): depression, grief, despair, shock
Moon + bouquet (9): happiness, fun dates, pleasure
Moon + scythe (10): break up, separation, emotional rejection
Moon + whip (11): sexual fantasies, erotic, sexual chemistry
Moon + birds (12): romantic dates, lovers, rendezvous
Moon + child (13): girl, fertile imagination, adolescent,
   pregnancy
Moon + fox (14): creative job, artistic gig, special effects work
Moon + bear (15): food, weight, eating disorders, financial
   speculations
Moon + star (16): prophetic dreams, space industry, coaching
Moon + stork (17): pregnancy, creation, self-empowerment
Moon + dog (18): romantic friend, mother figure, supportive
   relationship
Moon + tower (19): high expectations, delusions, psychiatric
   hospital, studio
Moon + garden (20): joyful times, entertainment, party,
   ceremony

Moon + mountain (21): longing, lonely, isolation, celibacy

Moon + crossroad (22): emotional instability, uncommitted, unsettled

Moon + mice (23): emotional distress, depression, anxiety, insecure

Moon + heart (24): in love, passionate romance, happiness

Moon + ring (25): marriage, commitment, creative contract

Moon + book (26): psychic knowledge, esoteric studies, creative project

Moon + letter (27): loving communication, designs, award

Moon + man (28): artistic man, creative, psychic, charming

Moon + woman (29): feminine, psychic, seductive, sensitive

Moon + lily (30): mature lover, parents, emotional stability

Moon + sun (31): attraction, love, chemistry

Moon + key (33): emotionally significant, spiritual insight, visions

Moon + fish (34): professional psychic, creative business, special effects industry

Moon + anchor (35): emotionally stable, long-term romance

Moon + cross (36): grief, emotional loss, spiritual crisis

Footnotes:

The moon is a strong emotional card showing feelings and emotions being shared between two people or about a situation. The feeling of falling in love is expressed through the moon card.

33- The Key

Keywords/meanings:

The key opens the door to life's mysteries. The card brings answers, solutions and success as it foretells that a major event is about to take place, maybe a twist of fate, an unexpected resolution to a difficult situation. This card is destiny at play and divine intervention into your life: pay attention to signs, clues and signals preceding the materialization of a wish or a miracle. The key wants to teach you about life's meanings and karmic lessons. It encompasses all the spiritual forces influencing our lives.

Descriptions:

A key person is a "key" player in your life. The influence of this individual is major and karmic by nature. The person will feel different to you as if you knew him or her in some way before you met for the first time (past life connection). The card portrays an outstanding individual who has a significant life purpose. He or she will probably stand out. Finally, the key is linked to all the green and blue colors of the spectrum.

Astrological reference:

The rulers of the key are Uranus (unexpected) and the North Lunar Nodes (destiny and dharma).

Associated Lenormand playing card:

Eight of Diamonds

Special features:

This card reveals if someone has a karmic connection with you and if you share some past life memories together. Therefore, it may foretell the coming or presence of a soul mate. For a "yes" or "no" reading, this is the card of absolute success as it is fate's design! The key is the connection to the spiritual realms in contrast to the cross which refers to religious beliefs.

Body connection:
The key is the third eye, the psychic center and in a larger sense, the Soul.

Card associations:
Key + horseman (1): spiritual signs, revelations, important encounter

Key + clover (2): synchronicities, fortunate incidents, positive twist of fate

Key + ship (3): significant spiritual voyage, destiny in another country

Key + house (4): spiritually charged home, feng shui, significant protection

Key + tree (5): karma, past life resurgences, spiritual experiences, insights

Key + clouds (6): spiritual confusion, lost soul, interferences

Key + snake (7): karmic lessons, challenging soul mate encounter, danger

Key + coffin (8): near death experience, dangerous path, spiritual break-down

Key + bouquet (9): harmonious spiritual life, spiritual clarity, artifact

Key + scythe (10): important spiritual decision, karmic transgression, karma

Key + whip (11): spiritual fighter or extremist, reincarnation, tantric sex

Key + birds (12): soul mates, karmic connections, spiritual discussions

Key + child (13): spiritual youngster, karmic child, angelic forces

Key + fox (14): important job position, key employee, agreement

Key + bear (15): philanthropist, organ donor, generous contributor

Key + star (16): significant life purpose, destined to be known, chosen

Key + stork (17): spiritual lessons, life changes leading to wisdom

Key + dog (18): soul mate, karmic 'family', counselor

Key + tower (19): spiritual organization, worldwide order

Key + garden (20): spiritual gatherings, karmic circle, metaphysical workshops

Key + mountain (21): delays controlled by fate, life long spiritual quest

Key + crossroad (22): free will, karmic journey, spiritual choice

Key + mice (23): spiritual depression, karmic ailments, past life interferences

Key + heart (24): soul mate, spiritual love, karmic relationship

Key + ring (25): spiritual marriage, karmic union, past life connection

Key + book (26): spiritual teacher, metaphysics, karmic lessons

Key + letter (27): important key documents, life changing news

Key + man (28): soul mate, significant person in your life, spiritual man

Key + woman (29): soul mate, influential woman in your life, enlightened

Key + lily (30): spiritual leader, father figure, enlightenment

Key + sun (31): life accomplishments, destiny, kingdom

Key + moon (32): prophecies, predictions, psychic messages, apparitions

Key + fish (34): spiritual business, key manager, recyclable products

Key + anchor (35): spiritual legacy, spiritual lifestyle, endless

Key + cross (36): prayers, mantra, religions, sacrifice

Footnotes:

This card says: "this is it!" Success is within your reach with divine support from the spirit realms– so go ahead and don't be afraid to pursue your dreams. Have faith!

34- The Fish

Keywords/meanings:
The fish relates to commerce and trade in general. Self-employment, freelance work and business activities are all elements of the fish card. In business it rules sales, import export, consulting and international exchange. This is the card of businesses and entrepreneurs, as it refers to independence and adventures.

Descriptions:
A fish person - male and female - is an entrepreneur, a business person, a consultant or a globe trotter. Self-made, usually the fish individual is savvy and independent. Physically the fish will often describe a man with dark grayish or dark brown hair who is well groomed and physically attractive. The eye color may be brown or hazel green.

Astrological reference:
The rulers of the fish are Jupiter (expansion) and Neptune (ocean).
The astrological sign is Pisces - water element - (February 21st to March 21st).

Associated Lenormand playing card:
Kind of Diamonds

Special features:
You can use the Pisces sign to predict a time frame. The fish connects with water which may point out to a lake, a sea, or a river, for example.

Body connection:
The fish represents the kidneys and the bladder.

Card associations:

Fish + horseman (1): new cash flow, new revenues, new employee

Fish + clover (2): business opportunity, fortunate business venture

Fish + ship (3): import export business, international sales, expansion

Fish + house (4): real estate business, mortgage co., fishing industry

Fish + tree (5): health or spiritual consulting, well-established business

Fish + clouds (6): odd/dysfunctional business, aviation industry

Fish + snake (7): problematic business, disloyalty in business

Fish + coffin (8): bankruptcy, closure, mortuary business, dissolution

Fish + bouquet (9): beauty/fashion related business, floral business

Fish + scythe (10): business decisions, down sizing the labor force, selling off

Fish + whip (11): physical fitness or sport related business, dynamic enterprise

Fish + birds (12): media based business, business partner

Fish + child (13): small business, children related business, start-up company

Fish + fox (14): surveillance business, independent contractor, sales force

Fish + bear (15): financial or nutrition related business, owner, manager

Fish + star (16): coaching, casting agency, aerospace

Fish + stork (17): growing business, production growth, expansion

Fish + dog (18): pet business, partner, consulting, fish and game

Fish + tower (19): judicial or hospital related business, luxury business

Fish + garden (20): network marketing business, customers, retail locations

Fish + mountain (21): nature oriented business, stagnant activities

Fish + crossroad (22): outlets, retail venues, franchises, offices

Fish + mice (23): business in trouble, down-sizing, losses

Fish + heart (24): charity business, passionate enterprise, matchmaker

Fish + ring (25): business contract, contractor, sales, association

Fish + book (26): accounting or teaching business, researcher, expertise

Fish + letter (27): business certification, permits, license, bill of sale

Fish + man (28): successful entrepreneur, independent, worldly

Fish + woman (29): business woman, consultant, well-traveled

Fish + lily (30): senior citizens related business, established business

Fish + sun (31): entertainment industry, competitive enterprise

Fish + moon (32): creative or advertising business, metaphysical services

Fish + key (33): life long business, vocation, charitable enterprise, locksmith

Fish + anchor (35): marine/boat industry related business, stable enterprise

Fish + cross (36): humanitarian enterprise, religious/nonprofit organization

Footnotes:

This card is the official symbol of any business or enterprise, but it does not represent corporate America. Large corporations and governmental bodies are better represented through the tower card.

35- The Anchor

Keywords/meanings:

The anchor refers to long-term goals, reliable situations and stable living conditions. It tells about courage, perseverance and determination as planning is necessary to achieve the goals. Settling down or reaching shores are reassuring attributes of the card. With this picture you may be building a legacy for yourself and your loved ones.

Descriptions:

The anchor person is confident, stable and faithful. He or she is supportive, consistent and reliable. The card brings a beneficial influence to the reading and predicts someone with a positive attitude. The picture may announce a man with dark features, sophisticated and self-reliant.

Astrological reference:

The rulers of the anchor are Saturn (stability) and Neptune (ocean).

Associated Lenormand playing card:

Nine of Spades

Special features:

The attribute of the anchor is an extensive time period, therefore it could refer to an entire life time. For example, marriages with the anchor are assured to be long-term and stable such as 10, 20, or more years. In terms of geography, the anchor symbolizes the beach, coastline communities and islands.

Body connection:

The anchor represents the hips and the pelvic bone.

Card associations:

Anchor + horseman (1): news, feedback, novelties, additions

Anchor + clover (2): prosperity, good fortune, constant growth

Anchor + ship (3): exile, emigration, life of travels

Anchor + house (4): family estate, inherited family home, final residence

Anchor + tree (5): healthy lifestyle, long life, resort living

Anchor + clouds (6): vagabondage, day by day living, instability

Anchor + snake (7): dangers, obstacles, challenges on the way

Anchor + coffin (8): life threatening lifestyle, end of a lifestyle

Anchor + bouquet (9): fun lifestyle, pleasant living conditions

Anchor + scythe (10): accident, sudden life changes

Anchor + whip (11): active lifestyle, abusive life conditions

Anchor + birds (12): companionship, partners, life long friendship

Anchor + child (13): childhood, courageous kid, stubborn

Anchor + fox (14): job seniority, life-long employment, loyal employee

Anchor + bear (15): living trust, annuities, life or disability insurances

Anchor + star (16): long-term goals, life time achievement

Anchor + stork (17): improved life conditions, better lifestyle

Anchor + dog (18): long-time friend, childhood friend, life partner

Anchor + tower (19): prison, government, institution

Anchor + garden (20): social lifestyle, life pleasures

Anchor + mountain (21): immobility, stalling, long delay, distance

Anchor + crossroad (22): 'on the road' lifestyle, adventurous life

Anchor + mice (23): deterioration, diminished lifestyle, stressful conditions

Anchor + heart (24): faithfulness, loyalty, unconditional love

Anchor + ring (25): commitment, long-term engagement or contract

Anchor + book (26): investigation, life long research, history

Anchor + letter (27): vital records, affidavit, will, living trust

Anchor + man (28): determined man, trustworthy, boat lover

Anchor + woman (29): reliable woman, established, beach goer

Anchor + lily (30): ancient, vintage, genealogy, records

Anchor + sun (31): fun life, resort lifestyle near or on the ocean

Anchor + moon (32): spiritual lifestyle, esoteric practices, emotional stability

Anchor + key (33): past life memories, karmic ties

Anchor + fish (34): life long business, fishing industry, marine company

Anchor + cross (36): lasting sorrow, painful life experience, religious lifestyle

Footnotes:

The anchor is an encouraging card to see as it tells you to continue on the path you are on. You will eventually reach your goals.

36- The Cross

Keywords/meanings:
The cross announces worries, concerns and pains. Unanswered questions may stay unfulfilled forever. The card contains sadness, guilt and suffering. Sorrow and despair may be expressed through tears, cries and prayers. Fate seems to be merciless. Some sickness may overcome you or just an uneasy feeling that does not go away. The symbol deals with guilty conscience and redemption as well. Thus, the cross symbolizes all the world religions.

Descriptions:
The cross portrays a depressed or sad person who is maybe sick, lonely or guilty. This individual could experience pain (physical or emotional), stress (life pressure) or despair (mental, emotional or spiritual). The physical appearance is to be looking fatigued and weak.

Astrological reference:
The rulers of the cross are Pluto (transformations) and Neptune (perceptions).

Associated Lenormand playing card:
Six of Clubs

Special features:
A religious person will appear with the cross verses a spiritual person may come through the tree or the key.

Body connection:
The cross symbolizes the lower back.

Card associations:

Cross + horseman (1): help coming, prayer answered

Cross + clove (2): hope, opportunity, positive turn of event

Cross + ship (3): wandering, exile, pilgrimage

Cross + house (4): chapel, church, temple, synagogue, mosque

Cross + tree (5): health issues, pains, incurable disease

Cross + clouds (6): worries, guilt, discomforts, spiritual depression

Cross + snake (7): critical issues, fears, out of control

Cross + coffin (8): grief, emotional pain, agony, suicidal thoughts

Cross + bouquet (9): relief, feeling better, recovery, healing

Cross + scythe (10): cuts, broken, injured, life-threatening accident

Cross + whip (11): physical abuses, injuries, sexual dysfunction, manic

Cross + birds (12): painful conversation, confessions, counseling

Cross + child (13): communion, baptism, birthing pains

Cross + fox (14): Red Cross employee, jobless, difficult job environment

Cross + bear (15): financial despair, charity recipient, protection

Cross + star (16): prayers, plea, faith

Cross + stork (17): relief, positive changes, recovery

Cross + dog (18): emotional support, rescuer, counsel, therapist

Cross + tower (19): hospital, cathedral, Vatican, religious headquarters

Cross + garden (20): group support, AA meetings, religious network

Cross + mountain (21): reclusion, social withdraw, monastic life, lonliness

Cross + crossroad (22): life crisis, painful dilemma

Cross + mice (23): anxiety, break down, depressive thoughts

Cross + heart (24): heartaches, emotional abuse, painful relationship

Cross + ring (25): forgiveness, plea bargain, difficult arrangement

Cross + book (26): religious artifacts, bible, Koran, religious texts

Cross + letter (27): painful news, sad announcement

Cross + man (28): religious man, worried individual, depressed, in pain

Cross + woman (29): woman of faith, anxious, in crisis, desperate

Cross + lily (30): passing, agony, aging pains

Cross + sun (31): great news, resolution, relief

Cross + moon (32): emotional depression, loneliness, sacrifice

Cross + key (33): spiritual depression, spiritually lost

Cross + fish (34): religion related business, refugees, charity

Cross + anchor (35): regrets, sadness, life long guilt

Footnotes:

The cross is an alarm that the soul is not at peace. It may not have any apparent physical sign, but its issues are serious, deeply affecting the individual's well-being. Support and counseling are advisable to help the person rebound from this kind of difficult period.

SECRET 2

How to Use the Cards

The original card lay out process and its challenges

The Lenormand cards can be utilized in any imaginable spread. Layouts – the way you place the cards to unveil the future, are just conventions you agree upon mentally to translate psychic information. You will find out that there are many layouts to choose from, too many to list here. I encourage you to always experiment. Trial and error will make you a better psychic. Conversely, I found out that rigidity to any one technique can detract from the ability to tap into the psychic mind. With time and experience, you may come up with the same conclusion that I did.

The only layout you should be aware of is a classic Lenormand referred to in many old European manuscripts. The classic layout involves using the entire deck and the 36 cards: the system carries many names, but it is basically a panoramic picture of the future within a year cycle. How to proceed with the classic layout?

To start, the deck is shuffled and cut in 3 stacks. Then you reconstitute the deck by putting the first stack on top of the second. And you finish by placing the one in hand on top of the third stack of cards.

The faced down cards are then placed as followed -from the first card on top of the shuffled deck to the last one:

```
  1   2   3   4   5   6   7   8
  9  10  11  12  13  14  15  16
 17  18  19  20  21  22  23  24
 25  26  27  28  29  30  31  32
         33  34  35  36
```

Once all cards are on the table you must flip all of them over to reveal their faces. Look for the keycards such as 28- man, 29- woman, 4- house, 5- tree and look through the book to understand the cards' meanings.

I highly recommended that you "charge" the keycards 28- the man, or 29- the woman, with first names, while you shuffle the deck to identify the characters in play in the panoramic spread. If you do not, it is harder to know what the cards are talking about and to whom they are referring. At the very least I suggest that the person you want to know about or whom you are doing the reading for - be it a client or yourself - should be "charged" into the corresponding symbol. This important step of "charging a card" is explained later on.

In order to read the panoramic spread, use the following steps:

> 1. Look for the inquirer, the person for whom you do the reading. Hopefully you remembered to "charge" the key card - man or woman - with the name of the person.

> 2. Observe the cards framing the keycard 28- man or 29- woman and interpret the meanings. Usually the cards in a square surrounding the keycard give character or physical descriptions.

> 3. Look for the other keycard which represents an individual. If this card has not been charged with a name, then it represents a stranger. However, if the dog card appears next to it, this person is then known to the inquirer.

> 4. Read the cards horizontally, vertically and in diagonal starting from each keycard. Do the keycards have cards in common? If yes, these cards may tell about the nature of their relationship or what may take place in the future between them.

5. Use keycards in the spread like the 4- house or 5- the tree to inquire about other topics such as health, home life, etc. The cards surrounding them give important information on those subjects.

I describe this technique in a simplistic way for the sake of understanding the basics. My book is not about teaching the panoramic spread. I will tell you though that this process can become sophisticated as many "characters (names)" may be introduced in one panoramic spread, <u>and</u> there are multiple levels of interpretation for those who master this technique. When you are good at it, you can elaborate on the subject's relationships, health, and finances.

The problem is that it is very time consuming and rigid. For example, you cannot ask questions to narrow down answers and you cannot see details about a subject if the spread does not give any. It is visually appealing for a client to see such a display, but it has not been constructed to provide detailed information on why events will happen this way. It only gives a glimpse of future, no more than that.

Nevertheless, by the time you have mastered this book, you will be able to test yourself with this tedious spread, and you may obtain interesting insights from it. In the meantime, you will learn my "free form" style of readings, a technique giving you more flexibility for psychic input and faster turn over to find answers.

Learning the "no layout" system

Nowadays people want answers fast! Clients want to get into the action and this "no layout" system will help you fulfill their needs. As you may have noticed already the deck is small and handy. The 36 colorful cards are easily shuffled and you should train yourself to manipulate them, to get comfortable with their size and feel.

Concentration and mental clarity are the keys to an excellent reading. A 'reading' is the proper wording for a psychic session. Your level of accuracy is directly linked with your ability to mentally block outside interferences such as noises, rambling thoughts and distractions. Consistent efforts in practicing with the cards and doing readings will increase your focus level over time.

Before you start any psychic session using the Lenormand deck, you need to know how to choose the correct keycard, the most important card in your spread, and how to charge it. If you read for a woman, you will choose the keycard 29- woman to represent that person. You need to "charge" the card with the energies of your female inquirer. In order to do this, you must concentrate on the keycard and associate it with her first name. This card has to become her. The same process stands for a man, but use the key card 28- man to represent him.

Knowing how to "charge" a keycard is a prerequisite before performing any card reading. A card is just a piece of paper with colors on it. Without the vibrations of your inquirer, it is empty and won't tell you or anyone else, anything. Our names represent our personalities and vibrations. Focus on the first name to personify your card 28- man or 29- woman, visualize the individual, tune in, concentrate and Voila! Your keycard has become the inquirer and you have successfully "charged" the card. The process is complete when you feel it is! Take advantage of the shuffling process to do this manipulation. No need to tell your clients about it. Some things are better kept secret.

Once you feel the card is charged with the vibrations of the person, spread the entire 36 cards, pictures face down, so you do not see them, in a fan position on the table. Be at peace and be clear. Postpone any reading if you do not feel like doing one or if you are very upset and can't clear your thoughts. When you are ready, while concentrating on your question or on your keycard if no question is asked, randomly start choosing cards. As you go, flip each one you pick over to reveal the pictures face up. Keep turning the cards over until you have found the keycard, and then add a few more cards afterward. Or you may stop when you have flashed on a specific card that calls you. If your keycard is another card such as 4- the house or 5- the tree, use the same process. At the end you should have cards lined up with their pictures up and the keycard among them. Then observe your selection carefully, listening to your inner-self.

Being open to your intuition is a crucial step in developing your psychic abilities. If you are a beginner, you will probably have to initially look up the cards' meanings in the book. But, before you do so, you should listen within. This step trains the brain to produce its own psychic language in whatever form it is gifted for: clairvoyance–visual, or clairaudience–audio, for example. Maybe you will feel or see something.

Only then should you go ahead and refer to the book for additional information. You can practice by doing readings on yourself. It is the hardest thing to do, but it is beneficial to promote insights and concentration. The better you get at listening to your intuition, the more effective you will be when reading others. Soon you will discover that reading for a stranger is so much easier to do. Little by little, you will develop confidence and memory of the cards' meanings without dependence on the book definitions. Remember this book is a teacher and a support, not a fortune teller. You are the psychic! Keep track of your insights by writing them down or by recording them on tape – my personal favorite.

The 5 step reading process

Use this guideline to help you provide a detailed reading:

1. Ask for all the first names of the persons you will be asked to do a reading on or for. If you deal with a common first name such as John and the person is not present, ask for their last name to better identify that person.

2. Ask your inquirer if she or he wants a general overview first. Some clients want to have their questions answered first or may have a topic that really bothers them, so you need to know what their motivations are early on. Clients should not be testing psychics. A good reading is evaluated over time, not on the spot. Some predictions may be over the top or perceived as impossible, though they happen months later. So do your best to make sure that your inquirer is honest and forthcoming before starting the reading. Deceitful clients make bad inquirers, distorting your inputs to fit their needs for validation.

3. If you start with a general overview, do not forget to charge the inquirer keycard. If your inquirer is a man, use card 28, if it is a woman the card 29 is perfect. Then, pull cards out of the spread until you have picked the keycard and add some extra cards after you find it. Interpret what you feel and see. Let your client know not to interrupt the flow of your words and insights. He or she can ask questions later once you are finished. This ensures that you won't be affected by clients' comments or reactions to your predictions, leaving you in a free space to tune into your psychic abilities.

4. Allow your client to give you feedback or to comment on your predictions. If the client came with questions,

address them one by one, like a detective. Use the 5 card spread or multi-level reading format explained in the next chapters as needed. You have complete freedom on how to draw your answers. Be creative and go with the flow.
If some information troubles you, re-ask the question or explain your dilemma to the client. Be honest if you can't see or feel something. Do not manufacture answers. Be cautious, if you're not certain. Keep in mind that you will never be 100% accurate. You will constantly make interpretation errors or miss some information.

5. Ask the inquirer to give you feedback on the reading in a few months so that you can assess your efficiency. As you read this book you will get to know what topics to be very careful about and how to limit mistakes.

SECRET 3

Predicting with Details

How to figure out time frames 'timing' for future events

You may have already noticed that each card can indicate an astrological sign, a season and that the number sitting on the top right of the card itself could be used in some ways. The key to giving accurate answers is to be focused on what you want to know. To estimate a time frame you need to focus on the "when" part of the question. Such as "when" will I go to Italy? Use your mind and utilize the following process while you shuffle the deck.

Focus on the prospect of going to Italy, visualize the trip, the destination and focus your attention in your mind's eye on a virtual calendar, while thinking on the "when." This is an important step. Do not rush this process, as it will negatively affect your accuracy. Beginners will take a very long time to get focused. Focus is a muscle of the mind that is used less and less these days. So be patient and persistent. It will get easier and the quality of your concentration will improve.

Now, once you feel clear on the "when" question, you can move ahead in choosing cards from the deck. Spread cards face down (pictures hidden) in a fan position, but without losing your focus. Pull several cards back to back (5 is a good number), and each time you pick one, flip it over to uncover the picture. You now have 5 'face up' cards. This is called a five card spread. Sometimes a card "jumps" at you catching your eye. If this is the case, look carefully at the card and its meanings (astrological sign, season, other timing features and so on). Observe the card immediately following the card for precision and to gain additional information (sometimes they come to support the initial card). It is the beginning of your answer, go with the flow and see what the message is...

It is possible that nothing calls to you, and this happens often. The reason could be a lack of real focus. Or, too many emotions are attached to the finality of the answer and they are clouding your "vision". Or simply put– no answer is available! Don't be defeated and try again. Refocus on the question, make sure you are calm and without distraction, and start again. It is likely that this time you will see an indicator.

It is all right to have a "do over" spread. You may have formulated your question in the wrong way and therefore the answer is not making any sense. Rephrase your question and start the process again. It is likely a clear message will appear.

Let's again look to our example: "When will I travel to Italy?"
No keycard has been selected prior to the reading. So we just have a simple 5 card answer:

20- garden, 33- key, 14- fox, 29- woman, 23- the mice

The answer is not that communicative to me. The woman card is not accompanied with a card that could be a time frame. So, I decide to ask again and re-do a 5 card spread. I refocus on my initial question by visualizing better my desire to travel to Italy. I reshuffle the deck and choose my cards.

The spread is as follows:

2- clover, **3- ship**, 32- moon, 24- heart, 34- fish

This time the card of travel, 3- ship, appears to confirm the topic of the question. It is always a good sign that you are on the right psychic path. The moon indicates a fast time frame (very soon) and the fish refers to Pisces time. From this association I deduct that my trip will be a happy one (very good ensemble of cards are present) taking place between February and March (Pisces).

This is a very simple example, but a good one to start your understanding of card associations. The following information relies on the same principals.

How to assess locations, physical moves and trips

The house card, the home, is the main symbol or – keycard – to look for in the spread. Focus on the question and on your residential location. This means visualize where you live at the present time. Think about moving, leaving that location to go somewhere. For example, I would like to know if I will be moving outside of Los Angeles anytime this year. I need to focus on the question and on my home and my desire to leave the town.

Again, I cannot stress enough the importance of focus and visualization. It is the key to psychic development and accurate readings. Choose any card, one by one, anywhere from the entire deck while you are thinking about your inquiry and flip each one face up as you go. Repeat the process until the house card- 4 appears, and then flip a few more cards after that. The cards you selected right before and right after the house are very important. Take the time to observe if one of those cards seems to indicate either a movement like the ship or the storks or the opposite like the mountain or the lily.

With regard to my 'move' question, here are the cards selected surrounding the house:

11- whip, 36- cross, **4- house**, 22- crossroad, 21- mountain

It is clear that the crossroad shows the hesitation and/or restlessness of my situation. "I am debating." But, the most powerful card is the mountain that stops any action to move. Translation: No, no move yet! It is not time!

Now, another example on the same question with a different outcome:

5- tree, 25- ring, **4- house**, 17- storks, 3- ship

I purposely chose a "by the book" type of answer, even if it is unlikely it will be that clear in your readings. But, for your comprehension it is good to have a perfect answer. The house with the storks is a classic move indicator, reinforced by the ship. My question was about leaving town, and the ship then confirms a long distance, which means it is likely to be outside of the area.

Now let's analyze the answers you may get when asking such a question:

No movement card appears nothing seems to indicate a move. What should you do? Take the time to redo the process. Just put more intense thoughts into the question to ensure it is not due to a lack of focus. If this happens again, then you should deduct that a move is unlikely right now.

The storks or the ship appear next to the house, but no extra details by other cards are given. Ask your question in a different way. For example, I would ask: "Will I move outside of Los Angeles soon?" Another way for me to have additional information is to ask: "Am I going to move far away from Los Angeles?" Rephrase your question if you don't get a straight answer. And then redo the reading.

The house is surrounded by many cards indicating changes and other information. The answer is you may move, but analyze the spread carefully to understand the interpretation and the message. Let me explain…

For example, with the same question "Will I move outside of Los Angeles soon?"

4- house, 32- moon, 22- crossroad, 17- storks, 3- ship

The moon is saying "soon," the crossroad shows "hesitation" or "too many possibilities," or timing could be "2 days, 2 weeks or 2 months". The storks confirm the move and the ship the distance, but the ship can also indicate March. Which one is the right time frame? It is very confusing, so let's break the answer down.

When there is more than one possible time indicator, you need to narrow it down by asking another complementary question such as: "Will I leave Los Angeles around March?" This way we can check to see if the ship was a time factor. The answer should be either a confirmation or a "yes" to validate March as the final answer or a "no" represented by negative, blocking cards. Or, instead I can ask: "Will I leave Los Angeles *within* 2 months?" Ask carefully. See how I used "within," which included 2 days, 2 week time frames, just in case the crossroad was a time card.

Though it is improbable I would move so fast I did not want to mislead the reading by limiting it with my thinking. I have seen impossible situations happen before, so I have learned to be careful before jumping to conclusions.

With regard to the question: "Will I leave Los Angeles within 2 months?" The answer should be either yes or a confirmation (it will take the crossroad to reappear again as an answer to confirm it) or a set of negative cards to say no, wrong question!

Here is the result of that question:

6- clouds, 36- cross, **4- house**, 7- snake, 25- ring

All these cards are quite difficult and with no indication of yes or confirmation of move. This does not appear to validate my question and therefore the timing of "within 2 months" seems to be inaccurate.

So I decided to try: "Will I leave Los Angeles around March?"
As you may have noticed, I made room for error in my question by using "around." It means that March should be considered a time

approximation in case it is not exact by then, although confirming that the move will take place around that time frame. If I had asked "in March," I may have received a negative answer, if the event was to take place April 1st!

The art of asking the right question can get tricky! You need to formulate your questions smartly and it takes practice. So let's see what the spread reveals with the question phrased differently.

Here are the selected cards:

5- tree, 26- book, **4- house**, 8- coffin, 10- scythe

The coffin means the end of that house particularly because it is being supported by the scythe (cutting off). It is a simple, but definite confirmation– saying "Yes, it is over where you live," and it should take place around March. Now, let's see if you have picked up the cards with a slight variation so that the answer leads to a "no."

9- bouquet, 17- storks, **4- house**, 8- coffin, 21- mountain

The mountain completely modifies the answer despite the presence of the storks. The storks stand before the house, and thus, it is not a confirmation of a move! This is simply the thought of a move. The coffin, which should indicate the end of the home, is being delayed by the mountain's stillness. Therefore, the timing is either too early or there will be delays with the move, making March an inaccurate time frame. We will have to try another approach to see when this move may take place.

Timing is challenging. Your intuition is the only tool for a decision, not your logic. A simple question may end up becoming a 20 minute work out, with 10 questions needed to determine an accurate time frame.

Now some additional information:

The ship- 3 and the crossroad- 22, indicate trips. The ship means traveling far, abroad, by plane or by boat. The crossroad is for road trips, excursions and exploration or "back and forth" type of trips. Sometimes the fish- 34 indicate traveling, but for business reasons.

Locations are described by the cards following the main key card so choose the keycards 4- house for moves, 3- ship or sometimes 22- crossroad, for travels.

Here is a list of different climates and locations that are connected with the following cards:

21- mountain: symbolizes mountains, valleys and hillsides. It
signals a cold and humid climate or rocky and dry conditions, if
associated with the sun for example.
34- fish: describes coastal communities, ports and islands. The
climate is humid, warm and tropical if the sun is present, but
with the clouds it may be cold.
35- anchor: goes with beach communities, the coast line and
islands. The climate is dryer than the fish with a milder
humidity factor.
20- garden: describes the country, flat lands and large spaces, or
groomed communities like Beverly Hills.
6- clouds: bring foggy weather, humid and rainy areas. They may
also refer to borders between two states or countries.
5- tree: announces forests, woods and shady areas.
19- tower: associates with big cities (capitals), condos and town
homes.
31- sun: means hot weather, deserts and dry lands like California.
22- crossroad: gives a sense of not too far, within driving distance,
or the next state line.
12- birds: indicates the next town, nearby, surrounding zip codes,
proximity.

3- ship: is about long distance, foreign countries, across the border, across the country.

30- lily: can be indicative of snow, very cold climate and northern areas such as Canada, Alaska or northern states.

How to describe an individual

When you need to know what a person is really about, you need to ask about their physical and character attributes. To do so, you first need to either use the "28- man" or the "29- woman" as your keycard to represent the person you want to know about, and focus on it.

For example, you would like to know who is going to be your next boyfriend. You must focus on the question in a way that you actually ask something more like "How can I recognize my next boyfriend?" You are looking for information describing this person, so make sure your thoughts go in that direction. Be a blank canvas with a complete open mind. Do not project what you would like or desire...the answer will be flawed.

I would like to give you a basic review of cards' meanings that unveil physical descriptions. Please use this list as a quick guideline and not as an absolute rule. For more detailed descriptions, check the chapter explaining the card's individual meanings.

1- horseman: well-proportioned individual
3- ship: dark haired person, manly male
4- house: squared physique, medium skin color, possible facial hair
6- clouds: dark/brown hair, highlights
7- snake: agile, flexible body, lean, long hair
9- bouquet: attractive, beautiful, blonde or light brown hair, great smile
11- whip: physically fit, sportive, sexy
13- child: younger looking, short height or petite
14- fox: freckles, reddish/auburn hair, small face
15- bear: strong torso, large individual, body-builder physique
17- storks: long legs, long nose, slim
19- tower: tall individual, long body
24- heart: pleasant looking, attractive, light hair coloring

30- lily: older person, grayish hair, senior individual
31- sun: charismatic, masculine look, blond person
32- moon: feminine look, charming, medium skin color
34- fish: darker person, dark hair, strong features

Now here is the basic list of character or specific attributes:

1- horseman: gentleman qualities (i.e. charming prince)
2- clover: optimistic, lucky, progressive
3- ship: foreign born, immigrant, international, traveler
4- house: family oriented, stable, protective, financially stable
5- tree: spiritual/religious, occultist, healthy, karmic, soul mate
6- clouds: moody, unstable, confused, dysfunctional
7- snake: felon, liar, trouble maker, jealous, manipulator, cheater
8- coffin: depressed, deceased
9- bouquet: lovely disposition, gentle, good nature
10- scythe: curt, mean, intolerant, decisive, judgmental
11- whip: active, sexual, manic, aggressive, cheater
12- birds: communicative, companion
13- child: immature, innocent, naïve
14- fox: liar, thief, deceitful, cheater, workaholic, sneaky
15- bear: strong, protective, controlling, caring
16- stars: idealistic, dreamer, creative, imaginative, independent
17- storks: on the go, can't settle down, unstable, nomad
18- dog: someone you already know, trustworthy, loyal, friendly, soul mate
19- tower: high morals, ambitious, condescending, noble, dependable
20- garden: popular, social, party-goer, promiscuous, charming
21- mountain: single, solitaire, lonely, abstinent, shy, distant, indifferent
22- crossroad: political, double talk, multiple lives, nomad
23- mice: stressed, nervous, sick, mean, negative energy, draining
24- heart: loving, caring, charming, altruistic, romantic
25- ring: engaged, married, unavailable, committed, secure

26- book: educated, graduate, informative, discreet, private, mysterious

27- letter: long distance, internet connection

30- lily: mature, peaceful, calm, established, experienced

31- sun: successful, powerful, egocentric, self-serving, attention driven

32- moon: spiritual, emotional, romantic, charming, famous, intuitive, creative

33- key: karmic, destined, soul mate

34- fish: entrepreneurial, business oriented, successful, international

35- anchor: stable, eager to settle down, established

36- cross: whiner, unsecured, religious, annoying, needy

Now let's apply what we have learned.

Let's ask: "Who is coming into my life for a love relationship?"

Spread the entire deck in a fan position -cards face down- and choose your cards non-stop until you have picked and revealed the 28- man – keycard – and add a few more cards after that. Remember to flip them over one by one as you pull them to show their pictures -face up-. Do not lose your concentration, stay focused on the question. Note that we use the entire deck until all cards are picked up or until we unveil the keycard. This is the "no layout" format.

Here are the cards chosen which surround the card 28- man:

11- whip, 16- stars, **28- man**, 1- horseman, 35- anchor

The whip associated with the stars turn the number 11 card into a positive attribute. We have the description of a sexy and attractive man with a good imagination and idealistic mind. The horseman indicates that he is well-proportioned, medium built with a stable outlook on life, as shown by the anchor, which in this case seems to lead to a possible long term relationship. This man most likely has dark hair with brown or greenish eyes.

Let's integrate our previous chapter on timing and ask: "When will I meet him?" Focusing on the profile we just unveiled from our first question about this man, we chose the 5 cards spread technique and these are the pictures:

4- house, 1- horseman, 21- mountain, 31- sun, 9- bouquet

Here is our first reading challenge:
Can you guess which card I am going to use as a key card?
The 1- horseman card has appeared before as a strong attribute for this new person. This is a strong male symbol and I felt it was the right card to take as a key one. But, the mountain delays everything in readings! It means I am going to have to be patient. The card can be talking of months or years. So how do we assess delays?

Before you get too familiar with your deck, you need to set a few mental conventions. These are internal rules, boundaries by which you will adhere to. For example, I am accustomed to doing short term readings. My brain is trained to search for only situations that will occur in the next few months, maximum a year. You too can create the same kind of conventions for yourself. You just need to establish these rules early in your apprenticeship. Once your mind understands that is the way you want it, the events will appear only within the time frame agreed upon at least 90% of the time. Sometimes a prediction will bypass your set of rules and that is because it is of serious importance. You should pay attention to these rare occurrences.

So to go back to my reading, I feel that this man will be coming into my life next year. The sun gives an indication of summer with the bouquet reinforcing the feeling of flowers and warmer days. But, look at the house with its number 4. April the 4th month of the year is the gateway to spring. My intuition leans to late spring, early summer time frame of the next year. The duet house and horseman give me an extra detail: this man is coming toward my house. Therefore, I know I don't have to look out there, this person will find me where I usually hang out, near my normal surroundings. The late time frame could be because he is not here yet...literally meaning not living in my town yet. Now I could and should confirm my findings by asking a question like "Will I meet my next significant relationship in the spring of next year?" And see if my insight is confirmed.

You now have learned a good system with which to profile and get details about an individual. If you wish to know more about someone you already know or have met, I advise you to use the "18-dog" card as your main card instead of the man or woman cards, but it is not required. The reason is that the man and woman cards are typically used to reveal an additional 'key' individual at play in the reading. The dog is typically used for people already known to us.

To know more about this familiar person you need to assign the card with the first name of the individual. By doing so you "charge" the card with the energy of the subject you are thinking of. Choose your cards while visualizing the person until you find the dog card and add few more cards after it. Start the reading with the dog card, like we used the keycards in our previous examples. You can now estimate the time frame of an event successfully and describe any person you need to know about.

Practice as much as possible and gain experience by reading for yourself and others. You will encounter difficulties and challenges. But, you will learn from your mistakes and with time you will improve—promise! The entire process we have just reviewed is very important to master. When you read for others, these inquiries are classic questions from clients. The more confident you are about your techniques and knowledge of the cards, the more details you can give. Do not hesitate to go back to the chapter describing each card in detail. Some cards have special features, and astrological associations that can be used in this section as well.

Note for students who would like to become professionals:
Be prepared to see interesting reactions from your "clients." For example, you may describe someone that they think they would never be attracted to...remind them that love is blind! You really never know who you are going to fall for—a wonderful quality of love. You will very likely experience the feedback from the "client" who is unhappy with your profiling because secretly he or she was hoping you would describe the person they already know or are smitten with.

"Clients" test psychics all the time, thinking this will ensure they are talking to the real thing. The problem is that they are taking time away from the real work of unveiling the future and in the end they just manipulate the outcome of their readings to fit their needs, most often to their detriment. It is a serious problem that does not have a solution. Human nature is to be emotional and clingy, even with people and relationships that are not nurturing. So be aware of this phenomenon and be truthful to your visions, even if your client may be a bit upset by not getting the answer he or she secretly wanted. I suggest you offer to look at the person they are interested in by focusing on the first name associated with a main card like the dog or the woman/man cards. Just tell the client what you really see, do not fabricate. If it is looking good, tell them, but if it is not forecasting a good relationship, let them know that too.

You must have integrity to be accurate. You are not a dream seller! Clients have to take responsibility for their inquiries. If they don't want to know what you really see for them, then they should not get a reading. I know it is a tough stand, but with time you will develop confidence in your abilities and hopefully you will be strong enough to refuse to compromise your work.

SECRET 4

Love and Romance

How to unveil an individual's personal life

You should be quite familiar with the deck and comfortable with the previous chapter before tackling this step. Practice by doing readings on yourself first to gain experience with the way the cards specifically talk to you. Do not read for a paying client until you have mastered all the steps.

To read someone's love life, I recommend you choose the woman or man cards as keys. Avoid using the dog as it needs to stay in the deck to reveal if this person already has a current love interest or an ex-flame still active in the picture. If you choose the dog as a key card you may see the man or woman card appears in the spread without knowing if this is a future love interest or someone already in the mix.

What cards indicate someone is single?

21- mountain: single and lonely, haven't been involved for quite some time
32- fish: independent single, too busy to be looking for someone
16- stars: optimistic single, hoping for a change in that area, dreamer
2- clover: happy single, take life as it goes, happy go lucky
3- ship: nomad single, does like freedom and traveling, may not be ready
30- lily: established single, likes life the way it is, too old to change
20- garden: single who loves to party, around people all the time, playboy

What cards show emotional instability which may create commitment issues?

22- crossroad: indecisive mind, can never be satisfied with one person
17- storks: can't stick with a situation long, looking for the next best thing
11- whip: sexually oriented, can't control desires, hunter mentality
6- clouds: mental confusion, manipulative mind, can be deceiving, cheater
23- mice: stressful personality, nervous, negative energy in everything

<u>Now an important rule to follow</u>: all cards picked before the support card or keycard represent the recent past or current situation. All the cards following the main card indicate possibilities of what is to come.

How should you use these significant cards?
Take as a keycard either the man or woman symbol. Focus on the card and charge it with the first name of the person you want to know about. Concentrate on the face, be visual for this exercise and when ready, start choosing your cards.

Let's do an example:
I just met John at a social event and I found him interesting. I am looking for someone who is available and open to having a stable relationship. I chose 28- the man card, as my key and I now visualize John as if I was looking at a picture of him. I associate his face and his name with the man card.

Shuffling the deck, I spread it in a fan position and start to draw cards one by one (flipping each one over face up) until I see my man card. Once found, I continue to pick another 4 cards. Here is what I selected:

18- dog, 24- heart, **28- man**, 20- garden, 25- ring

The dog and the heart show that John already has a romantic attachment. Why? Remember these two cards are coming <u>before</u> the man, therefore they are either the recent past or current situation. The garden leads me to believe this is not a committed relationship as the card signals an active social life and the ring reinforces the possibility of flirtations and other flings. John seems to have too much going on in the romance department.

Pay attention to the dog which gives you important information. There is no card indicating a break up, therefore the dog/person is still involved with John. This is a valuable detail on his availability and ability to be really committed in a relationship. John is definitively not what I am looking for!

Let's do another reading:
Jane wants to know about Chris, a man she met at her new job. Focusing on Chris' name and the man card, here are the cards that come up:

17- storks, 1- horseman, **28- man**, 34- fish, 32- moon

In this example, the horseman changes our basic reading rules: The card by nature represents a gentleman. We have to move our convention of a keycard from the 28- man to the horseman, making the storks the only card representing the current situation or recent past.

I know it can get complicated to understand but the horseman, this gentleman coming into her life -which just happened- can be associated with the man card "Chris" -because the cards are of the same gender- so the horseman can take the man card's place. Of course, this is an unusual situation. If the horseman was not next to the man card, ahead of it, we would not have made the substitution.

The storks announce changes. The horseman opens the door for the man "Chris" to come in. The fish is confirming he is independent, likely single, and in search of romance because of the moon. The moon is a "soon to happen" time frame. The fish represent the Pisces sign. Depending on when the reading takes place these information could be significant details.

So we can say to Jane that Chris is a likely romantic possibility (using the term "possibility" is wise, as she and Chris have free will in terms of starting a relationship). You can have a strong attraction for someone and still pass on the involvement, so be careful with your choice of words. Jane will know soon enough Chris' interest level, but for now, all indications show he is single and available.

Let's practice again:
Tom has a new girlfriend whom he likes very much, but feels her behavior is a bit strange. He wants to know what this is about.
Her name is Laura. Focusing on Laura and the woman card, here are the results:

24- heart, 26- book, **29- woman**, 22- crossroad, 18- dog

The love card shows the involvement between Tom and Laura, but the book brings a shadow of secrets. Tom does not know 'something' important about Laura, and a situation was likely already in play when they became involved (the heart and book cards refer to the recent past or a current situation for Laura). The crossroad is a bad sign, for it means instability or uncertainty concerning their involvement. Laura is on the fence in this relationship. Why?

The dog is the answer. Someone she knows is the other option in her life. Possible ex-boyfriend who came back in the picture? The crossroad usually reveals people who have double lives, compartmented relationships (like a wife-mistress-husband triangle). It is sad for Tom, but Laura is not fully into the relationship because of someone else she sees as well. This should explain the weird feelings he has experienced. Of course, I recommend you ask more questions to confirm the scenario described in your reading because you want to assure the maximum accuracy.

Understanding the outlook of a relationship

Can I marry this man? Does he love me? Is she the one?
All these questions are part of most readings and it is rewarding to
be able to answer them. In love and romance the true potential of
a relationship needs to be assessed quickly to avoid wasting time
and investing energy into a situation that won't bring you what you
want.

Let's look at the cards that usually indicate positive outcomes in a
start-up relationship:

25- ring: commitment, relationship, couple
35- anchor: stable, settling down, long term
2- clover: positive, progressive, happy
4- house: stable, family oriented, domestic situation
12- birds: couple, relationship, companionship
24- heart: love, romance, feelings
9- bouquet: harmony, happy, good relationship

Let's see in an example of reading how these cards work:
Sarah has been dating Paul for several months and feels much
attached to him. Her dreams of getting married and having
children are in full swing, but she is a little bit insecure. She would
like to know if Paul is thinking of her as marriage material. We start
to focus on Paul (his perceptions) and his view of the relationship
with Sarah. Therefore, our keycard is going to be the 29- woman
card, to represent Sarah, but we will analyze Paul's thoughts toward
that card (her). Again, focus... here are the cards:

16- stars, 18- dog, **29- woman**, 35- anchor, 33- key

The dog next to the woman card is very nice as it shows trust
and the feeling of knowing this person well. The dog refers to
companionship and friendship. The stars indicate that Paul sees
Sarah as a dream come true. The stability of the relationship is

confirmed by the anchor. Finally, the key seals the deal by assuring Sarah that Paul is definitively thinking about a future and a long term commitment.

Another situation for us to look into is James, who is crazy about his girlfriend, Jamie. He is a bachelor on a quest for the perfect partner and really sees Jamie as a perfect fit. But he is not sure of what Jamie feels about him, so he is asking for our help. We need to use the man card in this case as we want to see what Jamie, his girlfriend, thinks about the relationship. Remember to associate the card with the first name and concentrate on what you want to know. Here are the cards:

5- tree, 15- bear, **28- man**, 21- mountain, 6- clouds

The bear shows that Jamie sees James as a strong and protective man. The mountain may indicate his marital status which is single. The tree talks about a strong connection, even a karmic one. However, the clouds are not a good aspect because of their pairing with the mountain in the possibility area. Jamie is not sure if James is the man she wants to be with long term. Something is wrong and this may be a sign that she is not ready to settle down. Talking with James confirms their recent conversation about her desire to wait before walking down the aisle. She is apparently not ready to be tied down yet.

And here is one final case to study for more clarity with this chapter. Michael broke up with his girlfriend Angie. He is very upset because he believes the separation is the result of 'stupid' communication problems and he would like to know if the relationship is really over. We have two methods to answer such an inquiry.

Method Number 1:
We will use the woman card to represent Angie, and focus on the topic of Michael and Angie being separated and his question- "Is she is going to stick to her guns or come back?" So let's ask the

question "Is Angie leaving Michael for good?" With this angle, we will see what she is thinking of doing by using the keycard woman - Angie - and looking at the surrounding cards. We pick the cards until we find the keycard and then we add a few more. Here is the spread:

3- ship, 1- horseman, **29- woman**, 6- clouds, 35- anchor

The ship is her leaving the relationship. But, the horseman predicts a return, or come back. The clouds show a lot of confusion and a definite need for clarity and reassurance. The anchor confirms that the return may be permanent. Therefore, Michael can expect Angie's return and a good probability that their relationship can be worked on...and work out.

Method Number 2:
We will look at how Angie sees Michael by using the man card and focusing on her thoughts toward him. Same process, but we want to know about her intentions toward Michael. Here are the cards:

7- snake, 8- coffin, **28- man**, 32- moon, 2- clover

The snake shows problems in the relationship and the coffin reveals the end of it (the break up just happened). Would it be possible that this separation was motivated by pain? Did Angie end her romance because she could not stand the difficulties? The moon confirms that her feelings are not dead. She still loves him and the clover unveils her desire for a second chance with him. I guess they will be talking soon and probably get back together.

These two approaches can be combined for a more comprehensive look at a situation. It increases your chances for accuracy by understanding the underlying reasons of a decision or an action.

The commitment factor

When you get a request to look at a person, at a date opportunity or a possible relationship, it is advisable that you proceed through the following steps:

Step 1: If the question is about a real individual, use his or her first name to profile the person. The more you grasp someone's true motivations and personality, the easier it gets to predict their thoughts and behaviors.

Step 2: Assess the ability of the person to be stable in a relationship and review their past emotional history. You will be able to identify the unavailable person or the "already committed" individual. No point to invest in a married man, correct?

Step 3: Evaluate the potential between the inquirer (client) and the person he/she is asking you about. Some readings look great until this point: the client fantasizes on someone who may not be compatible with him/her, or the connection may be a love relationship that may not lead to a life commitment, like marriage.

If you are asked the question: When will I get married?
The keycard to use is the ring (marriage). Just focus on the question, while thinking of the person who is asking. Pull the cards until you get the ring and add few more. Let's look at this example:

20- garden, 33- key, **25- ring**, 21- mountain, 5- tree

Garden and key are good omens and indicate a happy celebration with a lot of people. The marriage will feel right (key- destiny), but the mountain delays every thing significantly (months or years).

The tree is pointing to its number 5. We can deduct the event in question won't take place for another 5 years.

Another example to help us understand timing is to ask the same question, but with a different outcome:

26- book, 1- horseman, **25- ring**, 32- moon, 9- bouquet

The book is what you can't see or know right now. The horseman talks about a situation coming soon. But, it also predicts a new man, and the book reinforces that you don't know him yet. The moon is always about romance, and it means a short time frame (soon).

The bouquet is a nice card to get, but the number 9 is probably the reason it appears in this spread. The reading seems to point to a surprise and a fast pace situation. It is possible that a wedding happens fast, within the next 12 months with someone completely new, soon to arrive! 9 could indicate the month of September or 9 months.

As you develop your psychic abilities and your relationship with the deck, you will get insights that will guide you in choosing the proper meanings. Practice and keep records of your predictions, so that they can be compared with the reality of your clients' lives.

SECRET 5

Business and Money

How to analyze career opportunities

What are the cards connected to business concepts?

14- fox: refers to all employees and people who receive regular paychecks. The fox is stability in employment and regularity in a schedule, with set hours.

34- fish: represent all business owners, self-employed individuals as well as consultants whose incomes are based solely on their performance, their talent or their business.

4- house: deals with small businesses, home business, small retail venues and small offices. The hierarchy is minimal and the business has few employees or none.

19- tower: portrays medium to larger corporations, legal firms, hospitals, courthouses, jails and any government agency. The White House, for example, will be indicated by the tower.

20- garden: can be linked to store chains, franchises or companies that have outlets everywhere.

22- crossroad: can point to part time activities, freelance jobs or extra side jobs.

15- bear: pairs with management positions, financial jobs with an insurance company or investment firm.

32- moon and/or 17- stars: are linked with creative work and artistic endeavors.

11- whip and/or 15- bear: can suggest the fitness industry, professional competitions and sports in general.

Let's do an example to understand how to answer work questions:

Donna is looking for a new job. She is a corporate executive and wants to get into a better position. Her question is: "Will I get an offer soon?" Focused on Donna and her question, we choose the fox because we are talking about an employed position. We spread the cards in a fan layout and start to pick and flip over cards as we go, looking for the fox. Here are the results:

17- storks, 22- crossroad, **14- fox**, 31- sun, 27- letter

The storks paired with the crossroad show an obvious sign of opportunities for change. There are two storks in the picture and we have two paths in the crossroad symbol. Could it be that she may receive more than one offer? It seems to indicate possible choices. The sun confirms success and the letter, a written format of communication, means a contract.

So to answer her question, I would say that Donna will be able to choose between several options and that success is the outcome. How soon may this occur? Well, we know that the crossroad can indicate 2 weeks or 2 months. The storks is a fairly fast pace card, so we can predict things will occur within a few weeks from the date of the reading.

Donna is ambitious and she would like to know if she will succeed in landing a better position than with her previous job. We focus again on the question thinking of the fox, and pick the cards. We have:

16- stars, 2- clover, **14- fox**, 12- birds, 17- storks

The stars represent our hopes and expectations -wishing upon a star- and with the clover reinforce the previous reading by acknowledging the positive change. The clover is about opportunities. The birds deal with positions such as when one assists a higher up, like being the right hand of an executive for example. But, the storks ultimately answer the question by showing progress and a move up. So, yes, Donna will be offered a higher position where she will most likely assist or collaborate with a powerful player.

Now, here is a question that often surfaces in readings for clients: "I don't know what career is right for me?" You can guide your inquirer by using these steps:

Step 1: First, ask the person to tell you if he/she has an idea of what would interest him or her. The reason is that you need to know where the client is coming from. Do they already have interests? Or, are they really clueless?

Step 2: Focus on the concept of a successful career: the question to have in mind while you pick the cards is "What career would this person be the most successful at?"

Do not forget that we have free will. You want to see what the most favorable path is for your client. But, ultimately, he or she has power of decision, and will determine what they want to do.

Let's do an example.
Mark is a high school graduate in his first year of college. He is not sure of his path right now. A smart, hard worker, he started to focus on a business path (degree), but he is having second thoughts on what ultimately his career should be.

Using steps 1 and 2, I focus on what he should be pursuing that will make him very successful. The cards I am looking for are the fish-business and fox-job in the same spread – both keycards. This means I will be looking at all the cards surrounding the fox and fish cards. I will likely have most of the cards of the deck lined up by the time I find both keycards. The keycards may be far apart from each other, so I choose to extract for my example, only the relevant cards surrounding each of them. We have the following:

8- coffin, 36- cross, **14- fox**, 22- crossroad, 21- mountain
and
33- key, 26- book, **34- fish**, 12- birds, 19- tower

The first set of cards show the fox surrounded by tough cards: the coffin and the cross show that Mark is not looking forward to having a boss and a regular job. The crossroad in this case means more instability than opportunities. The possibility for him to go through several jobs is very real. The mountain adds a feeling of emptiness and stops any progress. The option to move up the ladder seems bleak.

On the other hand, we have the second set of cards led by the fish: the key card points toward an important message, as the key sometimes does signify destiny. The book is about studying, but also about possibly working on cases that require investigation and discretion. The birds are communication of all sorts and the tower can represent big institutions. I feel it is likely representing a courthouse and I associate birds and tower as legal matters. This set appears to indicate that Mark is fit to become an attorney and to become a partner in a large firm.

As you progress in your knowledge of the deck and your abilities improve, you will start to use multiple layers of keycards in a single spread. This more complex use of the system allows you to give more details and to refine your answers in only one spread.

Understanding the future of a business

You first need to know if you are looking into a big corporation or a small 'mom and pop' type business. The tower deals with medium to large corporations with many employees. The fish represents smaller businesses with few or no employee and the house associates with retail business, and small offices. If the distinction is not easy and you need a short cut to speed the reading process, then choose the fish to analyze a business.

Let's do a reading on Paula who has a home business: she is a feng shui consultant. She has hit a rough patch lately and she would like to know if her business will pick up soon, and where I see it going in the next year. The fish is the keycard I chose in her situation, and I am going to do a double set by paying attention to the bear as well (remember the bear is money and cash flow for a business). I proceed, think of her question and I pick up the cards flipping them over as I go until both keycards are unveiled. Here are the cards:

24- heart, 23- mice, **34- fish**, 1- horseman, 20- garden

and

7- snake, 36- cross, **15- bear**, 32- moon, 25- ring

The heart reveals how much Paula likes what she does. But, the difficult times are indicated by the mice. The horseman brings new flow and good news, as the garden represents networks, clients, and people in general. No doubt that her business will pick up with more clients in the future.

Now the second set shows the snake and the cross with the bear. Her financial issues and her worries are clear. But the moon/ring combination predicts new orders or sales. The moon indicates a short time frame, so Paula's financial pressures should be over soon. Both keycards concur in their prediction.

Let's do another reading. Charles just opened a retail store in a cute part of town. It is his first business and he is understandably nervous. The name of his boutique is "Charles' Attic," and he would like to know how his new enterprise will do in the next 2 years.

I will now introduce you to the next level of reading with the Lenormand by using a triple set as follows:

<u>34- fish</u> will be representing Charles' business as a whole
<u>15- bear</u> will be used to look at his business cash flow and
<u>4- house</u> will be the physical representation of his store as "Charles' Attic."

Now I can focus on his overall business by thinking about the three main cards and spread the deck in a fan position. I will pick one by one until all three keycards have been unveiled. Here are the results:

16- stars, 23- mice, **34- fish**, 14- fox, 5- tree

and

13- child, 21- mountain, **15- bear**, 22- crossroad, 31- sun

and

1- horseman, 11- whip, **4- house**, 20- garden, 24- heart

Let's analyze the first set:
The stars with the mice show nervousness and anxiety over the new start up. The fish with the fox show a lot of work, long hours put into the store feeling sometimes like you are the employee of the business, but the tree gives it a healthy perspective. If Charles can work hard, long enough, then his business will survive its beginning stages and prosper.

The second set:
The child with the mountain tends to warn of slow movements. Because we are talking about money, this is letting Charles know that he is going to have to be patient. The cash flow will be small

to start, and will continue that way for a while. But, the crossroad paired with the sun indicates that a better financial situation will likely be coming about, and prosperity after two years is probable. Remember– the crossroad time indicator is "two."

Third set:
The horseman with the whip indicates action and information coming toward you. Here we are talking about the store represented by the house card. The whip has a positive influence, as it means repeat business, and the garden represents customers. The heart confirms the appeal of the shop and that a lot of clients will be back as they enjoy his store.

Often people come to you because they are experiencing financial difficulties. They are worried about their safety and their ability to cope with our demanding material world. You can forecast the future of an individual's finances or for a business, by using the bear as your keycard.

Let's review the basic meanings of cards we will be using in this finance category.

25- ring: is payments of all sorts
36- cross: is a warning card
7- snake: is about difficulties and problems
8- coffin: can represent the end of troubles or bankruptcy
26- book: can lead to audits, taxes and accountants
19- tower: may talk about lawsuits, IRS or governmental agencies
3- ship: means transfers
27- letters: are checks, money bills, etc.
6- clouds: are about instability and confusion
17- storks: announce improvements and changes
35- anchor: is stability, reaching objectives
10- scythe: refers to decisions
23- mice: indicate losses, debts and expenses
22- crossroad: points to multiples sources
21- mountain: shows delays, slow period, blocks

Let's practice:
Karen is 35 years old and she has had a bad divorce. Her financial situation is not in good shape, but she has been working to pay down her debts. She would like to know when she will be debt free and if some good news is on the horizon.
The spread is:

10- scythe, 23- mice, **15- bear**, 29- woman,
2- clover, 25- ring, 31- sun

I purposely extended my spread as there are multiple inquiries, and also because it is time to integrate a larger amount of cards so that you get more information. In this answer, the scythe and the mice do refer to her debts and financial demise. The scythe talks about the break-up. The woman card has appeared next to the bear. This means that the inquirer -Karen- is definitely concerned about the topic of 'finance' in her life. Because the first 3 cards stand on her left, they represent the past issues, so we know that there will be a shift soon. The clover means good luck, positive outcome. The ring shows payment of the debts and the sun the success as the reward. I will also use the clover as a time indicator -2-, so I would say to Karen that she should achieve her goals within 2 years.

Again, using multi-level readings helps get more information in less time. This technique can be used for any topic, as long as you are well-versed with the subtle meaning of all the cards.

The multi-level reading

Because we are getting good at this, let's increase the difficulty by doing a reading incorporating everything we have learned thus far – Mike and Jennifer are now living together. Jennifer came for a reading and she wanted to know if they will be able to fulfill their goals this year: they want to buy a house together and be able to get promoted in both their careers.

My choice of keycards is:
<u>4- house</u> to represent where they live and the next place they want to own.
<u>28- man</u> for Mike, to see where he is going with his life.
<u>29- woman</u> for Jennifer, to see what her direction is, as well.

Now I concentrate on what I want to know, thinking about each card and I visualize Mike and Jennifer, as well as their inquiries. At this level you need to be able to mentally compartmentalize each keycard with its purpose in the reading. In this example, after choosing the cards, it is likely the entire deck has been used in its entirety, and we have a long line up of 36 cards flipped over, pictures showing to reveal the three keycards.
Here are the results:

10- scythe, 4- house, 15- bear, 25- ring
and
30- lily, 28- man, 32- moon, 22- crossroad, 31- sun
and
35- anchor, 14- fox, 29- woman, 19- tower, 17- storks

For the first set, I only focus on one card (to the left of the house), because it is relevant, as the scythe is about the decision to let go or purchase a place. The bear and the ring confirm the purchase of a house this coming year for the couple.

For the second set, I kept the first card on the left, (you should always keep at least one card to reference the past), but what I am interested in is the future, not the past, so I keep the 3 cards on the right (future). The moon is a short time period. The crossroad shows multiple possibilities, and the sun success. No question that Mike is about to be offered great things very soon. The lily represents his professional experience, which may be valuable in the near future.

For the last set, I have 5 cards in a standard line up. The fox (job) appeared on the left, so I added another card on its left to show the past or current situation. The anchor and the fox show the stability of Jennifer's career. She has been with the same company for years. The tower indicates her promotion to a higher position, as confirmed by the storks. To summarize, Jennifer and Mike have nothing to fear: they will reach their goals within the year.

For every question you can use the multi-level spread as long as you don't get confused by including too many things. Simplicity sometimes is best. Certain questions won't do well with a multi-level spread. When you investigate a relationship the "simple question" system is better. But, for general business inquiries the multi-level can be very useful. Test and see which works best for your accuracy.

SECRET 6

Health, Children and Spirituality

How to answer health questions

This is a very delicate topic and you should be aware of laws condemning the illegal practice of medicine. Therefore, advice, treatments and anything related to medication or diagnosis (with regard to a client), when you are not licensed to do so, is reprehensible. Beyond good ethics, being sued by an upset family member of a client is not a situation you want to deal with.

Should you then ban any health related questions? No. But you must explain clearly to the client why you are not there to diagnose his or her sickness, and advise your client to consult a physician for medically related answers. In the meantime, you can give them a description of your insights on the subject. In this chapter I will reveal how the Lenormand cards apply to health questions without censorship. But I urge any apprentice and professional to be very cautious in answering them.

Readings are supposed to be for entertainment purposes only. But if you would like to venture into this sensitive field, your client must inform you if he or she has been diagnosed with a specific disease. It would be up to you then to decide if you are comfortable doing a reading on the subject. I do recommend you stay away from serious conditions and explain to your inquirer that it would be inappropriate for you to perform any health reading. Again, you do have the right to refuse such inquiry.

Now the process to forecast a health condition is no different than all the other topics covered previously. You rely on a keycard and you concentrate on the life force of the inquirer, while picking up your cards. The keycard in health is the tree. You need to pay attention to its surrounding cards. The ones on the left of the tree indicate situations already in effect or in the past, verses the ones on the right, which will predict the future. Some cards are very helpful in analyzing a person's health:

21- mountain: refers to blockages, immobilization. This card appears when people suffer from chronic constipation, if a part of the body is not working well or if they have been in bed for long period of times.

11- whip: recurring ailments, allergies, stubborn pains, and restlessness.

6- clouds: warn of problems that are hard to diagnose because of a variety of symptoms. Health instability will be the result of this symbol.

12- birds: signify therapies of all sorts as they deal with verbal communication, and therefore, listening.

26- book: predicts tests being necessary, investigation of the problems or hidden issues not yet apparent. You should examine the other cards near it to understand what the issues may be.

8- coffin: announces clinical or temporary depression, a major change in the health condition, usually for the worse. Sometimes it can indicate the end of an illness. You should always pay attention to the cards next to this one to know how to translate the meaning.

7- snake: is the problem card. It usually means that your client may get sick with a common disease such as flu, cold and so on. Look at the surrounding cards to confirm the warning.

36- cross: tells about anxiety, worries and physical pains

23- mice: talk about emotional and psychological anxiety causing pain, stress and worries. These problems can manifest themselves as physical ailments.

17- storks: always predict health improvements.

14- fox: reveals a health issue that is still "hidden," and may cause ailments, but not strong enough to alarm the person. Because the card may warn against a more serious illness, I advise that you refer you client for a check-up with a medical expert.

32- moon: deals with emotional and hormonal problems. It is a cycle; therefore it could indicate a health problem that repeats itself regularly.

10- scythe: is usually a good indicator for a possible surgery or a mechanical action performed on the body such as dental work, laser, extraction or biopsy.

15- bear: corresponds with the digestive system, food habits and tumors from any origin. Again, always double check your answers by performing several spreads on the same topic and send your client to their physician if you have a 'bad feeling' from this card.

25- ring: is a diagnostic and treatment with a high rate of success.

19- tower: represents a hospital or a medical facility.

27- letter: is a prescription, a test result or an X-ray.

18- dog: personifies a doctor, a healer or a therapist from any background.

The issue of predicting death needs to be addressed. It is impossible to know accurately when a person will die due to illness. The coffin can sometimes indicate a radical change which could be a "passing" but, I found out in my practice that it takes more than this card to make me think of death. The ship in certain circumstances, can give me more concerns if it is paired with the coffin, and if the diagnostic is not good to begin with. I have seen this combination being a prediction of someone's final departure. However, I do not advise that you venture in that direction, even if the client wants you to. Remember, the future can change with the right treatment, the right specialist and the right attitude.

Fertility and birth

A lot of women are curious and will frequently ask fertility and birth questions. You can address fertility by focusing on the key card 13- child, and by choosing cards until you find it in your spread. The surrounding cards will give you some hints. See the example below:

Olivia just got married and she is thinking about having children. She asked how many she and her husband may have. The cards appear as follows:

4- house, 16- stars, **13- child**, 35- anchor, 22- crossroad

The house and the stars show her hopes and the stability in the marriage. The anchor has 3 fork parts and the crossroad means two. My deduction is that Olivia could have 3 children, and 2 may be twins.

Let's do another example:
Sarah is 45 years old and she has not yet found anyone to be a life partner. She wants to know if she could still have children, as she contemplates having a child on her own. Concentrate on the child card and Sarah's question, here are the cards:

7- snake, 10- scythe, **13- child**, 32- moon, 17- storks

It is clear that the answer warns of some problems because of the snake's presence. But, the scythe is a good omen in this case, as it gives the clue of some mechanical intervention done to permit pregnancy. Indeed, the conception is confirmed by the 3 cards: child, moon and storks. The moon adds a short time frame. My response to Sarah is that she will probably do some in-vitro fertilization and that it will be successful the first time around. The possibility of more than one embryo is indicated by the storks (2 birds).

You can also check the fertility of a woman or man by using the tree and the child in a multi-level reading. For example, Genevieve has been trying to get pregnant without success. She is concerned about her ability to have children and she would like me to check her situation. I have to concentrate on what I want to know: first the female health and its fertility which is represented by the tree. At the same time I need to see if any child is in the future. Here is the result:

24- heart, 21- mountain, **13- child**, 1- horseman, 25- ring
and
11- whip, 23- mice, **5- tree**, 2- clover, 16- stars

The first set shows how much the child is wanted (heart), and the delay is clearly marked by the mountain. But it seems that the horseman brings some good news because the ring is a "hit."

The second set brings stress and sexual activity around the issue: the whip is sex and the mice stressful situations. The clover brings opportunities, second chances and the stars are your dreams come true. My deduction is that Genevieve is stressing over the entire process of getting pregnant. Reminding her to relax and not make it a big deal is essential. The clover talks about the gambling odds. Therefore, what it really comes to is to reassure Genevieve that it is going to happen as it is confirmed by the horseman with the ring. But that stressing over how long it takes may be the reason why she is not pregnant yet!

Some pregnant women do ask about their pregnancy, and the process of delivering the baby. If you are comfortable doing health readings, you can share some positive insights regarding how things may unfold. Use the meanings at the beginning of this chapter.

Let's do another example:

Madeleine is having a difficult pregnancy. She needs to rest a lot and she wonders if the labor is going to be hard as well. Focus on the tree (health) and the fact it is for a baby, so keep the child card in mind when you pull your cards. Here they are:

32- moon, 22- crossroad, **5- health**, 6- clouds, 15- bear
and
1- horseman, 11- whip, **13- child**, 9- bouquet, 19- tower

The first set talks about her moodiness, her hormonal fluctuation through the moon and crossroad combination. The clouds confirm her discomfort and the bear her body increasing weight.

The second set shows the horseman and the whip predicting a labor soon to come and because both of those cards have a certain speed, we can relay that it will be a short labor. The bouquet demonstrates a happy outcome and the tower represents the hospital she will be staying at. So fortunately, Madeleine will not have to endure a difficult birth and it should go as planned.

Sterility can appear in certain readings like in this following example. Sherry was asking a general question about children and here is the answer:

3- ship, 25- ring, **13- child**, 23- mice, 6- clouds
and
20- garden, 29- woman, **5- tree**, 7- snake, 26- book

The ship and the ring show Sherry's desire (wanting to have a child), but the mice and clouds give no promise of one. The garden, the woman and the tree show her healthy, but the snake and the book indicate difficulties in her desire to conceive, and the need to investigate the problem.

This is a perfect example of how we can change her future by giving Sherry this information. Indeed, if Sherry follows the reading's advice, she may discover what her problems are and remedy the situation. In that case, it is likely her reading will have a different answer once the issue is resolved.

You do not have to do multi-level readings for questions like these. Actually, I usually separate them and use the deck completely for each question. The reason is that I like to double check an answer particularly if it is a sensitive topic. I want to make sure I interpreted the signs properly.

So I usually start by checking the woman's ability to conceive and then her number of offspring. Or I will do the reverse. Sometimes the answer about how many children is quite interesting. The reason is birth control. Women now have control over their reproductive abilities and some spreads may show it like this one:

24- heart, 15- bear, **13- child**, 20- garden, 25- ring

The heart and the bear show a loving and motherly aptitude. The garden's meaning is "many" and the ring confirms the fertility. Tough isn't it? I think that the message means she can have as many children as she wishes! So how many is up to her.

But, try one more time on the same question to make sure. If you get something like this again, then the answer stands. I need to relay to you that some female clients may not understand this type of "vague" answer. Children are not anymore a fate thing, as women have choices and this will surface in readings. Take the time to explain the increasing amount of free will we humans have nowadays. Fortune telling is not what it used to be. The future is mostly created with our current choices and decisions. We make it up as we go, and clients need to understand this modern aspect of 'fate.'

Finally, the question of the baby's sex is going to be asked. Predicting the sex of the unborn is not my forte, I must admit! We all have our strengths and weaknesses. Your odds are 50-50, and I wish you better success in this area than I have experienced. When you need to find out the sex, focus on the child card and pick until you find it. Look at the cards surrounding it. Some are more feminine, some are very masculine. Depending on the energy that you feel, this should give you a sign of who is to come – male or female. Good luck!

Uncovering past life connections -soul mates- and karmic lessons

I will remain brief on this topic as this could be the subject of another book all by itself. The notion of soul mate needs to be demystified: we do have many soul mates that are more or less closely intertwined with our souls. Our closest soul mates are usually our parents and our children, rarely our life partners. This does not mean that we have good relationships with our closest soul mates. Most of those connections are intense and difficult.

We are raised by our parents who teach us lessons in life and we leave them to create our own experiences. We then have children to teach life lessons to, so that they can leave us when the time comes to create their own path. Soul mate meetings are about soul evolution and human growth through the cycle of union and separation.

A very close soul mate does not stay with us. He or she comes to teach major lessons, but will leave when the time comes regardless if you have learned the lessons or not. We have a karmic appointment with that person, set up a long time ago before incarnation, and we meet again to help each other evolve through specific experiences. Some are happy ones, most are difficult scenarios. We recognize that soul mate by the way this person behaves, dresses, and says things to us.

We don't know why, but we are attracted to that individual, and we can feel the telepathic connection. That is the sign of our karmic connection, recognition between two souls of a previous relationship. These past karmic lives could have been very diverse such as parent-child relationship, lovers bond, slave-master link or murderer-victim story.

The tree represents karmic ties, spiritual connections. The dog symbolizes a soul mate, someone we knew from previous lives – past life.

To see if someone is a soul mate just focus on the first name or the full name of the person. Use the corresponding woman or man card to personify him or her. Focus on the spiritual link between you and this individual. Flip the cards until you find the keycard and then observe the surrounding symbols. If the tree or the dog appears near, then you know you have an active karmic situation and that this person is here to change you and your life in significant ways. The outcome can be good or bad. It does not matter. What is important is *what* you have to learn from this person.

Some clients want to know what their past life was with this person. The way to approach this question is to focus on the other person's name and to think of the tree. Ask about your life connection, your previous story. Flip the cards and look at what the tree is surrounded by.

15- bear/32- moon: can represent a mother, a grandmother, a female care taker.
30- lily can personify a father, a grandfather or a father figure.
13- child means a youngster, a young adult.
11- whip connects with a lover or a fugitive.
19- tower represents captivity.
10- scythe shows accidents.
34- fish symbolizes a boss or a master.
4- house may indicate a land lord, a king, a title etc.
12- birds talks about friends, companions.
21- mountain refers to isolation and celibacy.
22- crossroad and the ship foretell stories of travels and exile.

Finally 18- the dog, refers to a close soul mate, which has been physically recognized by the inquirer as if it was an old acquaintance.

This example will show you how to use the man and woman key cards together to find out the karmic connection between two people of the opposite sex. If you are doing this reading for two people of the same sex, then you will need to use the woman card with the dog (2 women) or the man card with the dog (2 men). Oliver has met Hanna two weeks ago and feels he has a special connection with her. He would like to know if this new relationship will become significant.

I use the man card for Oliver and the woman card for Hanna. I pick the cards until both cards have been unveiled and look at all those standing between the two keycards. Remember to focus on what you are looking for: the nature of the connection between the two. Please be aware that there can be many cards standing between the key ones so if you get overwhelmed by the number, redo the reading by asking for a simplified answer. It usually works. The dog or the tree must be present between the two keycards to qualify the two people as soul mates.

Here is the spread -all the cards below should be placed in a straight line-:

11- whip, **28- man**,
9- bouquet, 20- garden, <u>5- tree</u>, 26- book,
29- woman, <u>18- dog</u>

This spread needs to be read in both directions to get an idea of each person's position. Oliver is an attractive man as shown by the whip (sexy). The bouquet gives him a nice personality and a physical appearance that draws a lot of attention (garden=popularity). The tree indicates a karmic link between Oliver and Hanna confirmed by the presence of the dog right next to her: the soul mate, the person you knew from a past life. The book informs us that he did not know her in any way, until meeting her and that he still has to get to know her, (of course, he met her two weeks ago).

Now let's look at Hanna with regard to Oliver, so we need to start the reading from the right to left: Hanna is a loyal and friendly personality as the dog signals. She is educated (book), and spiritual (tree). She sees Oliver as a well-balanced person (garden and bouquet) and people seem to like him very much. The whip shows that he appears sexy and fit to her. The spiritual connection maybe felt by Hanna as well -the tree is present between them-, but it is more obscure for her, as the book stands in front of the tree, hiding the knowledge of their connection.

When you work with spiritual relationships you should be aware that not everyone believes in soul mates or past lives. Therefore, sometimes one person feels a connection, but won't qualify it as a past life memory either because he/she doesn't feel it that way or because he/she does not share this belief.

You will notice negative cards connected with the tree or the dog sometimes. These symbols inform you that there will be problems in that relationship. Close soul mate connections can be as difficult as a parent-child relationship. If the situation is too hard, the two people involved won't stay together. It does not mean they haven't fulfilled their karmic obligations to interact with each other. It is completed. But, learning and evolving are free will decisions. One may not want to tackle these lessons and decide to remain at the level one started. Humans do have choices. They can learn and grow spiritually or they can remain stubbornly at the same level in the course of their lifetimes. The important point is to be given the opportunity to grow, thanks to the encounter of a soul mate.

As you can see the Lenormand deck can be used for mundane questions or for much more spiritual inquiries. Experiment with the cards and keep track of your findings.

SECRET 7

How to Improve Your Psychic Abilities

How to choose the right Lenormand deck

You should spend some time browsing the net and look at all the existing artworks available. Choose the cards that call to you or the design you feel most comfortable with. If you can not make up your mind on two different styles, buy them both. Once you have them in your possession, learn to enjoy gazing at each card in order to become familiar with the symbols. Observe each card's unique details, and feel the colors. Eventually you will bond with one style of cards. Keep the deck and start to work your way through this book by practicing with your set.

In my psychic career, I have enjoyed the same Lenormand deck version for more than 20 years. The "no poem" cards of AGMuller allow me to avoid any possible distraction: I discovered that the poems tend to tease clients' attention and consequently my concentration, during a clairvoyant session. My aunt and my grandmother -both Lenormand experts- liked the Carta Mundi version with either the French or German lyrics. So really, no deck is better than another. I have in my personal collection 6 different styles. The affordability of this oracle makes it easy to own.

The most popular little Lenormand are:

- Le petit jeu Lenormand from Carta Mundi (Belgium)
The Carta Mundi deck is known for the poems printed on each card. The original lyrics were in French, but the publisher offers them in German and English as well. Depending on your choice of language, the artwork will differ accordingly.

- Le petit jeu from AGMuller (AGM Switzerland)

With a different design than Carta Mundi, French and English poems are available as well as a rare "no poem" version, a very popular set among professional psychics (lyrics replaced by playing cards). The artwork remains constant regardless of the language you choose.

- Petit Lenormand from Piatnik

These cards don't have poems, but instead playing cards are displayed in the logo (an identical system to the J. Muller "no poem" version). The design is similar to a painting, creating a softer feeling.

- Lenormand Tzigane

The design possesses an East European flavor -Gypsy style- with a somber artwork.

- Lenormand oracle cards by Gina di Roberto from Lo Scarabeo (Italy)

The simplified pictures displayed in an antique style make this artwork shine without any other distraction (no lyric, no playing card is displayed).

- LS French cartomancy deck from Lo Scarabeo (Italy)

The deck is close to the 19th century original publication and features the playing cards. It is in an antique style with simplified graphics.

- Mystical Lenormand by Fiechter/Trosch from AGM Muller Urania (AGM Switzerland)

The most intricate Lenormand deck ever, with new detailed artwork and interpretation, Harry Potter style! This beautiful and sophisticated version has added features such as astrological symbols.

- Lenormand deck by Erna Droesbeke (Netherlands) available on Schors.nl

This recent version offers a different interpretation of the Lenormand with a New Age style: soft color combinations and modified symbolism topped by the playing cards motif bring novelty to the deck.

The following websites carry most of the Lenormand decks published since their creation:

- Magicka.com

The number one metaphysical website in the world -located in Belgium- sells the traditional and latest deck versions like the Mystical Lenormand, some interpretation books, and other Lenormand tools. The English and French sites provide full-color viewing of the cards, quick e-mail responses by multi-lingual staff and international mail orders. The website is interactive with games, music and provides the most comprehensive retail venue for the metaphysical arts.

- Amazon.com

A great website to browse regularly for books on the Lenormand deck and to purchase cards like the Gina di Roberto and the LS French cartomancy versions. The site updates its inventory often and their fast shipping as well as excellent customer service makes it a premier venue for the Lenormand deck.

- eBay.com

A significant contributor to the Lenormand's international recognition, eBay features sellers who auction antiques, rare versions and new decks for sale. The Piatnik version for example, is regularly featured on eBay, making it a good place to search for a Lenormand deck.

Here are some additional secrets that you may find helpful to improve your psychic relationship with the cards.

The 10 psychic commandments

The conditions in which you do psychic readings, regardless of the tools you use, are very important. These commandments should help you increase your insights and limit your mistakes in interpreting them. The following are guidelines for any psychic apprentice.

1- Choose a day for readings when you feel balanced and open.
If your emotions are out of control because of an upset or hard day, postpone any oracle as your mind won't be able to utilize its abilities. You can use meditation or soothing background music to help you relax, but if you are still unsettled after 15 minutes, please do cancel.

2- Do not drink alcohol, smoke or use drugs before or during a session.
This is common sense because these activities are known to affect your brain's abilities, but I still see professional psychics crossing that line every day. Shamanism uses herbs to promote hallucinations for spiritual insights, but the problem is that you will loose control over the reading. You need to direct your mind to logically shape the session so that you uncover all possible details. This requires a control over your insights, and your questioning. I know that if I have a glass of wine and try to do a reading, my psychic abilities will be affected and my insights foggy.

3- Use a special place to perform your sessions.
You need to create an environment conducive to calm and harmony. Noisy, messy rooms are counterproductive. The use of candles, aromatherapy, soothing colors and soft lights promote a spiritual aura. Velvet cloth on the reading table helps preserve the deck over many uses.

Pets should be kept away, particularly cats. They love jumping on tables to get your attention, but this can become intrusive and break the psychic flow. Children should not be attending a reading–with no exceptions. For example, babies are very sensitive to vibrations and are always very tight to their mothers. Even a profoundly asleep newborn will wake up within 10 minutes of a session as it senses the shift of the mom's energy toward another person.

4- Your sessions should not be offered free of charge.
It is tempting to give away your services for free, but I would advise against this practice. If you do not wish to charge money for your efforts, you should at least ask for a trade or a donation of another nature. My aunt used to ask for flowers, eggs, vegetables, and car lifts, instead of money. It is important that your inquirer respects your time. Please set boundaries on how long your session will last. Working for 3 hours on someone's future and getting a coffee in exchange is not a fair trade, so know when to stop!

5- Allow people to record your words.
Unless you are relaying "sensitive information," it is beneficial for you as well as for the client to provide the option of recording the session. Accuracy is measured over time in readings, not at the time of the consultation. Writing down what is being said is an alternative, but not as exact as a voice recorder. The client will be distracted trying to write down your words and may omit important details he or she does not think relevant at the time. I even took the step of allowing people to bring along a friend. Friends are great for thinking up questions your client won't or can't think of in the moment– it is called psychic amnesia, and they are good witnesses later on.

6- Refuse service to co-dependents and abusive inquirers.
Please be aware that there are individuals out there who are selfish and self-centered: they will use and abuse you because of what you can "see". If someone keeps asking the same question over and over without listening to your answers, then you should step up and refer this person to a therapist. Anyone treating you without

respect should be shown the door. Good clients bring good referrals, but an abusive, mentally ill client won't have friends to refer! Losing such a person will allow you to have more time for the true seekers, the ones who really need your guidance.

7- Readings should be for entertainment purposes only.
The reason for this disclaimer is to prevent people from using psychics as a substitute for qualified professional help. If your client has health questions, he or she should be asking their physician. It is also true for people who have severe depression, and/or serious psychological issues, which makes them in need of therapy. So please refer your inquirer to specialists, therapists, lawyers etc. You will have the opportunity to build a great network of highly qualified people, and in addition you will also gain the respect of both your clients AND professionals. Be a responsible service provider by knowing your limits.

8- Learn to switch on and off your abilities.
By creating a ritual before any session you are sending a signal to your brain to get into the "psychic mode." This helps to establish a switch for your abilities to turn on and off, and to allow you to be free of residual vibrations after you are done with a reading. When you switch "ON," your psychic antenna deploys and you are fully focused. When you are done with a client or for the day, you switch "OFF," and your brain can relax and you can step out of your altered state of mind.

A ritual can be 5 minute meditation with a white light surrounding you. The meditation will protect you from negative energies, followed by the client being asked to say his/her name and birthday for example. You invent and modify your own introduction until you feel it works to get your mind to switch at will. The more you practice the more aware you will feel that there is a switch. People who tell you they can't turn off their abilities are not professional psychics, but amateurs, who are still learning. Professionals have to have that on/off button for their own sanity. This comes with experience and many, many readings later. Once you are finished with your work a simple thought "it is over, job is done" can be an OFF signal for the brain. Or you can create a "closure" ritual in a same style as you have established your "intro" one. I can switch on at will. It takes me just a few minutes to get into my 'ON' mode. Thus, when I am in 'OFF' mode, I am really off. The ability to regulate is the key to a balanced, healthy psychic life.

9- Avoid reading children and teens.
The reason I am opposed to giving these youngsters readings is because they do not have free will yet! They are dependent on their parents, do not usually earn money, and therefore can not change their situations. Young minds can easily be disturbed and manipulated, and therefore your readings could present a danger to their well-being. On the other hand, I am perfectly at ease with giving parents readings about their kids, as it often promotes better parenting and understanding.

10- Communication with the dead should be left to those who are naturally gifted with this special talent (mediums).
Losing a loved one is a very painful emotional experience for a human being. The grief is such that finding a person who can connect you with the departed is very much sought after. But, it is a serious service to provide, and should not be offered if you have no talent for it. A medium is usually a person who knows he/she has the gift early on. You don't improvise this specialty, you either are a medium or you are not. My strength is not in this field so I usually turn down any inquiry in these matters unless the client insists and understands this is not my strongest suit. Again, disclosure of your limits and boundaries is absolutely crucial in the business of foretelling.

The following techniques should help you enhance your abilities. Experiment and you will certainly get better over time.

The 3 visualization techniques you should know

These visualizations are simple but effective in promoting balance and psychic visions.

1- The "white light" preparation
Visualize yourself bathed into a white and pure light surrounding your body, like an aura, with the source coming from above. See it bringing peace and comfort. Feel its energy entering the top of your head, down to your feet, like a shower of positive vibrations. Hold this image for a few minutes or until you feel your mind calms down. The protective white light plays like a shield against negative energies brought by clients, entities and others. Use this technique before starting any reading. I highly recommend this exercise to bring balance to chaotic thoughts and emotional disturbances. It centers the soul and prepares it to mesh with others.

2- The "movie theater" visualization
Imagine you are sitting in front of a large theater screen, and think about the question you want an answer to, or the person you need to know about. See the white screen right ahead of you and relax your mind without drifting away. You will initially see shadows and vague pictures coming onto the screen. That is good! After a few minutes, stop the exercise, even if you were unable to see clear images. Repeat the exercise on a daily basis, a few minutes at a time (no more than 10 minutes at the beginning). Over time, your visions will get clearer and more detailed. This visualization improves clairvoyance and focus of the third eye. As you train, you will notice progress in your ability to concentrate on daily tasks without being distracted.

3- The "open message" technique
Imagine your brain displaying a pair of antennas like an insect does. Visualize yourself tuning in like a radio, to the invisible waves around you. You may experience a tingling sensation, a vibration on the top of your head. Feel the wave of energy going through

your body and be open to the experience. Stay quiet, and calm, while you sense the room around you. Pictures may flash into your mind. Messages may come to you. You can use this technique while pulling cards. This exercise improves your channeling abilities. Mediums are individuals who can tune in to communicate with people who have passed on. Channeling is communicating with entities that may have no previous earthly incarnations, such as spiritual masters. Be aware that at the beginning these sensations may be frightening, as you may experience the feeling of something mixing with you. But, if you use the white light visualization before starting this exercise, you will be protected against any negative entity or low vibration being.

Becoming psychic requires daily exercise and dedicated practice. Like an athlete who trains for the gold medal, you should be patient and consistent with the process. Gain experience by taking some classes, and read some books in order to try different techniques. The more you learn about the spiritual realms, the more empowered you will feel.

Feedback

Accuracy is a way to know where you make mistakes and what your strengths are. You won't remember all your sessions, nor all your clients. So have them write down your predictions or record your readings. As you progress, their feedback will help you gain the confidence and the experience you need to deal with a paying clientele.

No one is right on all the time about everything. Too often you will have clients who do not understand that notion. Please take the time to educate them on the reality of this work. Very good psychics are usually about 80% accurate on average. Time is difficult to predict, as it has been created by humans. The Universe does not work with our calendar year or months, but by synchronicities of energies.

The notion of Destiny is an interesting concept. I do believe we come to this earth with a plan. A few things are set in advance because they are important for our purpose. But, most of our situations are based on free will. What we choose to do today will create our future. We must take responsibility for our decisions and stop making excuses for our complacency. Seeing the future allows us to make better choices, and in doing so create a happier life.

CONCLUSION

The Lenormand Empowerment

The Little Lenormand deck is an investigative tool utilized to look deep into events and situations that sometimes haven't revealed all their facts. It is a lie detector, an oracle, and a psychological mirror to unveil important information. Unlocking its secrets gives you the ability to see future possibilities, and upcoming events so that you can negotiate your next steps.

The cards need to be learned and manipulated with regularity, and after a while they become part of your soul. At that moment, your talents take over and you enjoy your own connection with the deck. New meanings and new images will be coming through based on your own life experience and psychic abilities.

This book is a door to an exciting relationship with the cards. For the beginner, it is an introduction to the Lenormand deck, for the intermediate student a constant source of vital information, and for the expert, an esoteric reference to the Lenormand oracle.

Personally, I look at the little Lenormand deck as a good friend, who is there in times of need and happy to help when I ask. I sometimes don't like what it has to say, but the oracle has always shown me an accurate glimpse of the future.

Once in your hands the deck will faithfully tell you the truth, so that you can make the right choices for your own future and help your loved ones navigate around life's challenges. With this new found wisdom you will become the master of your own destiny!

ABOUT THE AUTHOR

Sylvie Steinbach is an international psychic, karmic astrologer and life coach. Her successful practice is located in Los Angeles, California. Recognized as a leading expert in the Lenormand deck, Sylvie decided to share her vast knowledge of the cards by writing one of the first contemporary English guides.

"The Secrets of the Lenormand Oracle" is her first self help book to teach people around the world how to use the divination deck created by Mademoiselle Lenormand.

You can contact Sylvie through her website for private sessions, Lenormand workshops, and special appearances.

www.sylviesteinbach.com

Made in the USA
Lexington, KY
11 April 2014